Essentials
of Emotional
Intelligence

Also by Dr. John Demartini

The Gratitude Effect
The Productivity Factor
The Resilient Mind
The 7 Secret Treasures

Essentials
of Emotional
Intelligence

Dr. John Demartini

MEDIA

Published 2024 by Gildan Media LLC
aka G&D Media
www.GandDmedia.com

ESSENTIALS OF EMOTIONAL INTELLIGENCE. Copyright © 2024
Dr. John Demartini. All rights reserved.

Front cover design by Tom McKeveny

Interior design by Meghan Day Healey of Story Horse, LLC.

Library of Congress Cataloging-in-Publication Data is available upon request

ISBN: 978-1-7225-0656-8

10   9   8   7   6   5   4   3   2   1

Contents

Introduction

*This is the true joy in life: Being used for a purpose
recognized by yourself as a mighty one, being a force of
nature instead of a feverish, selfish little clod of ailments
and grievances, complaining that the world will not devote
itself to making you happy. I am of the opinion that my life
belongs to the whole community and as long as I live, it is my
privilege to do for it what I can. I want to be thoroughly used
up when I die. The harder I work, the more I live. I rejoice
in life for its own sake. Life is no new brief candle to me.
It is a sort of splendid torch which I have got hold of for
the moment and I want to make it burn as brightly as
possible before handing it on to future generations.*

—GEORGE BERNARD SHAW

What is your emotional intelligence? Can it be
increased? If so, how?

Your *Emotional Intelligence* (EI), or your *Emotional Quotient* (usually abbreviated as EQ to parallel *intelligence quotient* (IQ), is defined as the ability to wisely perceive and interpret your sensory reality, respond accordingly and wisely, and use the "appropriate" feelings or emotions for effective and respectful communication, leadership, social development, and other objectives and responses.

Whether you know it or not, your day-to-day behavior is impacted by and governed by your unique individual hierarchy of values. Your perceptions, attentions, intentions, goals, or objectives that are most meaningful, useful, and important to you, are all determined by your unique set of values or priorities. Your evolving hierarchy of values continually influences how you interpret and respond to your environment. Through certain brain processes, which I'll discuss later, you filter your reality and sensory perceptions and monitor your motor responses in accordance with those values.

Think of a mother walking through a shopping mall. If her highest value is her children, she's likely to notice store products relating to her children. She'll filter out or overlook other items that are less important, such as those related to possibly business or sports. Her unique hierarchy of values and their associated brain processes will filter her reality to include and exclude different perceptions, even though she may not be consciously aware of this selective process.

In the same way, when you meet someone, two processes take place in your brain:

Your body's peripheral nerve-based sensory receptors constantly take in transduced information from the environment and transmit it to your central nervous system, or spine and brain. This is called sensory *reception*.

You also have subconsciously stored emotional experiences based on what you have previously perceived as pleasurable or painful—to be sought out or avoided. These subconsciously stored experiences are imposed on the new or current information taken in by your senses, resulting in your *perception*—which is generally biased and polarized as something to impulsively seek or instinctively avoid.

These subconsciously initiated seeking impulses and avoiding instincts originate deep down in the subcortical survival-oriented part of your brain. They generate quick, almost instantaneous responses before you can consciously think about them. This process is fundamentally useful, inasmuch as quick impulses towards or instincts away from perceived supportive prey or challenging predators can be essential for survival. Although you may need those responses in an emergency, the number of life-threatening moments that you will encounter are more likely to be minimal. If you perceive a current object or individual that reminds you of a highly charged event in the past, you can over emotionally react in a way that is less than ideal and in some situations highly distractive to your greatest fulfillment. It is wiser to learn to be more neutral, adaptive, and resilient, to realize that the perceived threat was most probably just a false alarm, and to center or recenter yourself. This ability to calm down or dampen the extreme survival reactions is a sign of emotional intelligence.

You may have seen this happen in your own life—a time when you overreacted with an emotional response before you have even had the time to think it through. You may have judged yourself harshly for that reaction because it conflicts with your notion of how you are ideally and socially "supposed" to be, resulting in emotions stacked up on top of other emotions.

An individual who is more moderate and neutral and has more balanced ratios of perceptions awakens the cortical executive center in their forebrain, which regulates or dampens their lower subcortical impulsive and instinctive emotions. This higher center is there to calm and neutralize previous emotional perceptions, making them less likely to overreact.

Emotional intelligence is simply the process of wisely and objectively managing these impulses and instincts so as to serve your greatest interests in any situation.

Individuals who can moderate their emotional reactions are considered to have a high emotional intelligence: EI or EQ. They do not let the external world permanently run them, but simply and more wisely use their initial reactions as feedback to master or govern their lives.

The quality of your life is based on the quality of the questions you ask. Questions that make you aware of information you may have ignored or been unconscious of help you become fully conscious. This, by the way, is what your intuition is constantly urging you to do: it is constantly trying to take your EQ to a higher level.

When your EQ is high, you more efficiently and effectively move into a fully conscious and balanced state: you are inspired by your life, living by purpose, and extracting meaning out of your experiences. In fact, your capacity to extract meaning itself points to a high EQ. When you extract meaning out of your existence, you're able to see events as they are rather than as you initially and subjectively projected and assumed. The more traits, actions, or inactions you can reflectively and equally own within yourself, that you initially judged as existing more or only in others, the less the world around you will be able to push your buttons and initiate ungoverned or extreme emotional reactions.

When you can ask the question: "How is whatever is happening to me *on* the way, not *in* the way?" you tend to awaken your forebrain's cortical executive center instead of your lower, reactive, subcortical brain. In this state, you will become more grateful and demonstrate an elevated EQ.

Anything for which you cannot feel gratitude for is baggage. Anything for which you do feel gratitude for is fuel.

The ability to ask questions, equilibrate your mind, and bring yourself back into a poised state is true emotional intelligence. It also allows you to have reflective awareness and true empathy because you realize that what you see in others is also equally inside you. As a result, you can understand and more effectively respect others. You can be less reactive and more receptive to them, because you understand that you share the same behaviors. You're also likely to have equity between you and them and equanimity within yourself, which allows you to be authentic and inspired.

If you want to be loved and appreciated for who you are, this is the way to do it.

By equilibrating your perceptions of others and your-self, you can liberate yourself from the impostor syndrome, or the false facades, masks, and personas you wear, and you get to be the true, more inspired and powerful *you*.

Your emotional intelligence enables you to break through and break free of your impulsive and instinctive reactions and live more in accordance with your highest values and with your own true nature. It allows you to be truly liberated from your many overreactions.

Let's go more deeply into this adventure.

1

Wisdom beneath Chaos

Let me start by going back to when I was seven and in the first grade. I was told by my first-grade teacher, Mrs. McLaughlin, that I would probably never be able to adequately read, write, or communicate, never amount to much, or go very far in life, because I had learning disabilities, dyslexia, and a speech impediment.

At that point, I was given a dunce cap to wear, along with Daryl Dalrymple, another challenged student, and labeled a dunce. By age thirteen I left home and became a street kid while struggling to endure staying in school. At age fourteen I finally dropped out of school. I continued as a street kid and became a beach bum surfer. I lived in Freeport, Texas, part of the summer and hitchhiked to California and down into Mexico at age fourteen. At age fifteen, I went over to Hawaii to surf the North Shore. By age seventeen, I was surfing full-time. I hadn't done much if any reading, but an experience of strychnine poisoning and a subsequent encounter with a remarkable teacher named Paul C. Bragg entirely changed my life and my perspective and trajectory. He helped me identify what I deeply wanted to do with the rest of my life: to overcome my learning challenges and someday become intelligent and to study universal laws as they relate to mind, body, and spirit, and particularly healing. I wanted to be intelligent enough to be a teacher.

The night I met this gentleman, I had an epiphany and saw in my mind's eye a new, inspired vision, which led me to became incredibly driven to overcome my learning challenges and later become relatively intelligent, and a scholar and a world-traveling teacher. I wanted to know the universal laws—the laws that apply in all different areas of life—and how they relate to self-mastery, human behavior, achievement, and healing.

Shortly after meeting Paul Bragg, I flew to Los Angeles and hitchhiked back to Texas, where my parents were living, sat for and miraculously passed a GED high-school equivalency test, and fulfilled the other requirements for entering college. I started to apply myself and gradually and painstakingly learned how to read and learn.

Starting with memorizing thirty words a day taken alphabetically from a Funk and Wagnalls dictionary and growing my vocabulary by properly spelling and pronouncing them, understanding their meaning and using them in a sentence, I then gradually began devouring other dictionaries and encyclopedias and every great classical book I could get my hands on to learn new words and their meanings. I wanted to know the laws of the universe. That meant everything to me. When you're told that you'll never read, write, or communicate (as I'd been told in first grade) and later discover you actually can, you want to catch up and thirstily know.

When you have an illness and you almost die, you want to know about life, death, and wellness and how to maximize your potential. I started to apply myself and began to build momentum and eventually excel until I became one of the top students in Wharton Junior College, where I was able to rebegin my formal education.

When I was eighteen, with the help of a group of dictionaries, I began to try to read a book sent to me by my uncle Ralph, written by Gottfried Wilhelm Leibniz, the seventeenth-century German philosopher, who, among other achievements, was the coinventor (with Isaac Newton) of the calculus.

The first chapter of Leibniz's book *The Discourse of Metaphysics* was about perfection. What he termed, "Divine Perfection."

The more we come to know and understand God's works,
the more inclined we shall be to find them excellent,
and to give us everything we could have wished.
—LEIBNIZ

Leibniz said that there was an underlying order in life—or as physicist David Bohm later called it, an implicate, enfolded, deeper, more fundamental order, as some physicists still say today. There's an underlying magnificence, an underlying symmetrical and mathematically elegant beauty, an underlying divine order and love that exists in the universe. Unfortunately, few people ever grasp this great truth: most are walking around oblivious to this underlying hidden order and live within an outer sea of apparent chaos and uncertainty.

According to the late mathematician, engineer, and scientist Claude Shannon, the father of information theory, disorder represents missing information, or what some psychologists called the unconscious, and order represented no missing information, or the fully conscious. Entropy, or the tendency to disorder, randomness, or uncertainty, measures the amount of information missing—the missing or hidden variables. Negentropy, or the tendency to life and order from disorder, measures the wholeness or recollection of the missing information—full conscious awareness.

As I read this chapter in Leibniz's book, I got grateful and inspiring tears in my eyes. Its subtle truth touched me deeply; I understood that there was somehow a higher hidden order and wisdom underneath the apparent chaos in mundane life. At that inspiring moment, I dedicated my life to finding a way to unveil this "divine perfection" and hidden order in the apparent chaos. The term *divine* is ultimately derived from the root *div* meaning *to shine, to illuminate, to emanate excellence, to awaken, to enlighten,* and it refers to the essence of our most authentic being within, the intrinsic and essential source of all of our individual existence that drives our spontaneous and inspired action and that makes us illuminated and wisely knowing.

Leibniz said the divine perfection and order permeated every being (or, as he put it, *monad*). Furthermore, every human being has access to this underlying implicate order. But most people are fooled by their outer sensory impressions and perceptions; distracted by these partial hallucinations or illusions, they're unable to recognize and awaken, or attune to, this order. They are too distracted by their lower animal-like impulses and instincts and subconsciously stored misinterpretations of their outer misperceptions.

That took me into investigating what is called the philosophical *logos*. This refers to the intelligence, knowledge, or logical reason and order of the universe, the emanating mental-spiritual field of consciousness—the infinite potentiality by addition or subtraction or by multiplication or division, as Aristotle and more recent authors such as Erwin Schrödinger, Thomas Nagel, and Deepak Chopra have called it—that appears to permeate the world and universe.

According to the ancients, this logos was in a sense a state of mindful enlightenment, or as the Persian philosopher Mani, the founder of Manichaeism, described it, a particle of shining light. According to the Neoplatonic philosopher Plotinus in the third century AD, each of us is like a particle of light or emanating light of our soul. We are particles of illumination, so our real nature is a part of that reasoning or enlightening logos.

Logos has another sense as well: it means *study* or *inquiry*, and it is divided into different studies, which are called the *disciplines* and *ologies*. Anyone who would explore the ologies and had the discipline to integrate them into their thinking would eventually return to the reasoned, ordered, and enlightened logos. This enlightening inquiry is what led me to be polymathic and relentless in my pursuit of learning and knowing, particularly in the field of human behavior.

With the continued help of dictionaries and encyclopedias I set out to identify all of the then known ologies that a human being could explore or study, and I wrote them all down. I wanted to know the common essence of these ologies, because I felt that somehow if I could find the underlying more enlightened order and principles that governed all of them, I might understand the fundamental law within the great logos, which would allow me to be a more valuable teacher.

I started to explore all these different ologies to find a common thread in them and understand how it links to a more awakened and inwardly governed human consciousness. How does it relate to healing, wellness, and wellbeing? How does it relate to the development of the psyche and genius? How does it relate to love and wisdom—*philosophia*? How does it relate to a self-mastered, or well-governed and ordered life? How and why does it have such meaningful implications in the exploration of emotional intelligence?

The First Law: Quanta

Along the way, I came across the quantum mechanics world. Again with the help of dictionaries and encyclopedias, I devoured *The Principles of Quantum Mechanics* (1947), written by Nobelist Paul Dirac, and discovered the significance of light quanta and their corresponding generated and annihilated subatomic particles and antiparticles as well as their brief or extended dynamic interactions with atomic matter. This book awakened a thirst for applying quantum principles to ever larger structures, including correlations with the human brain and mind.

This next small section may be a bit more technical than the remainder of this book, but I believe it is still important and meaningful enough to include in this chapter.

The term *quantum* goes back to the twentieth-century German physicist Max Planck, who said that discontinuous particles, or quantitative essences, underlie all existence. In short, the energies of the universe come in packets or particles known as *quanta* (*quantum* in the singular).

The quantum was also previously discussed by Aristotle in the fourth century BC in his *De anima* (On the soul), but it was only formulated mathematically later by Planck at the beginning of the twentieth century.

First, no doubt, it is necessary to determine in which of the summa genera soul lies, what it is; is it "a this-somewhat," a substance, or is it a quale or a quantum, or some other of the remaining kinds of predicates which we have distinguished?
—ARISTOTLE

This is one of the major universal principles: both the human psyche and the human soma of the dualists and the mind/body integration of the monists come in the form of quanta as well—that is, minimal units, or monads.

Leibniz believed that each human body had one dominant monad, which controlled the others within it. This dominant monad was often referred to as the essential and enlightened soul.

Although the brain, mind, or psyche is a whole, it is composed of multiples of these quanta—monads or minimal components. As a result, the psyche also grows and develops by quanta. Erwin Schrödinger, another major developer of quantum physics, in his 1944 book *What is Life?*, proposed that life or consciousness evolved by quanta or quantum leaps. The Swiss psychiatrist Carl Jung and the Austrian physicist Wolfgang Pauli discussed a similar conclusion.

Let's look at this concept in terms of the human body. We have a whole body, which is made up of systems—the nervous system, the endocrine system, the cardiovascular system, and so on; there are about a dozen systems in all. Each system in turn is broken down into its various organs, which are composed of tissues. The tissues are broken down into cells, the cells into organelles, the organelles into molecules. The molecules are composed of atoms, which in turn are composed of subatomic particles. These subatomic particles are associated and resonate with specific wavelengths of light, so our body is really composed of neutral biophotonic units of energy or light and electrically charged particles of matter, including atoms, molecules, and complex molecules.

In fact, all of our cells have photoreceptivity: they respond to light. Each of us is a collective receiving and broadcasting system of light; we're made of solids, liquids, gases, and atomically stored, absorbed, or emitted light. We are composed of light resonating matter that is also receiving, communicating, and broadcasting light. We possess photoreceptivity, biophoton communicativity, and bioluminescence: we take in, respond to, communicate through and give off light.

Our communicative biophotons appear, though faintly, within the visible spectrum, running from near-infrared through to violet, or between 200 and 1,300 nanometers. Besides optical communication, there appears to be a whole other level of operation in the brain that appears be on a previously undiscovered entangled quantum level.

Our brains, with billions of neurons, convey billions of biophotons per second. This mechanism appears to be sufficient to facilitate transmission of a large number of bits of information, and may even allow the creation of a large amount of quantum entanglement.

For individual quantum communication links to form, a larger quantum network with an associated entanglement process involving many distant spins—the nuclear spins interfacing with different axons—must interact coherently. Some scientists believe this entanglement process underlies consciousness. And a strong preservation of entangled photons has been found propagating in brain tissue. In addition to quantum light particles, there also appear to be transient mathematical entities called virtual photons and virtual particles.

In mathematics, virtual particles only briefly exist. Quantum theory predicts that every particle spends some time as a combination of other particles in many possible ways. Quantum mechanics allows, and indeed requires, temporary violations of conservation of energy, so one particle can become a pair of heavier particles (the so-called virtual particles), which quickly rejoin the original particle.

Every high-energy photon light particle will spend some time as a virtual electron plus its antiparticle—the virtual positron—since this is allowed by quantum mechanics as described above.

The fields formed out of these virtual photons, the intermediating particle/waves of the electromagnetic force (light), are deemed by some scientists to be the carriers of organizing consciousness in the brain.

The universe is composed of atoms and their subatomic quantum particles: about 75 percent hydrogen atoms and another 24 percent helium. The rest of the elements in the periodic table make up the remaining 1 percent. Being made up of atoms, the universe is also composed of a vast number of quanta, particles of light, photons, or radiation and virtual photons and particles. The universe, like our bodies, is therefore basically made up of visible light, or invisible radiation and visible matter or invisible matter, as well as virtual photons and virtual particles.

In this light and in these virtual particles and atoms, there is potentially an underlying intelligent information base, a field of organizing intelligence, which some philosophers and theologians have called the *logos*. Everyone is or has a parcel of that logos; our brains are receiving and broadcasting systems for communicating with and transiently storing it.

The logos can be expressed through higher frequencies, the most awakened state of intelligence, but it can also be expressed through lower frequency tunings for expressing a lesser degree of intelligence. So we have the ability to tune into both higher and lower frequencies of intelligence through cortical and subcortical portions of our brain, which involves simultaneous and sequential contrasts of perception—what the Greek philosopher Empedocles called *love* and *strife* or *judgment*.

The speed with which we perceive both sides of an event determines the intelligence frequency. When we perceive both sides simultaneously and have full consciousness, which psychologist Wilhelm Wundt called *simultaneous contrasts*, and which quantum physicists might call a superposition, this represents a higher frequency (love). When we perceive both sides sequentially over time, and we have conscious and unconscious portions of awareness, at any one moment, which Wundt called *sequential contrasts*, this represents a lower frequency (judgment)—an incomplete awareness. The former is more objective, reasonable, and neutral, and the latter is more subjectively biased, emotional, and polarized, but entangled.

According to Michelle Frank, writer of the article "Hidden Variables behind Entanglement" (published in *Scientific American*, April 2023, p. 45):

> Abner Shimony, a philosopher and physicist, called entanglement "*passion* at a distance." Entanglement offers the wild notion that once certain particles or systems interact, they can no longer be described inde-

pendently of one another. What happens to one, no matter how far it may travel from its entangled partner, instantly affects the other, as decades of evidence now shows. The characteristics of entangled particles are correlated, without any apparent communication, and at any distance. What's more, each member of the entangled pair seems to lack a complete set of definite properties until the moment when one partner is measured. Then, instantly, the entangled pair will be in sync—even if the particles have drifted galaxies apart. It's the ultimate star-crossed *love*.

According to quantum physics, photons and real subatomic and virtual particles can exist in multiple states and even multiple locations simultaneously—a state called *superposition*—until the moment they are measured, or perceived. At this moment one particle of the pair—up—becomes consciously perceived and the other, the complementary antiparticle, becomes unconscious but entangled—down.

Simultaneous
Whole
Enlightened
Fully conscious
Authentic Self
Superpositioned
Spin up
Conscious of + / Unconscious of
Exaggerated Self
Pride

Inauthentic Self
Entangled complementary opposite selves
Endarkened
Shame
Parts
Minimized Self
Sequential conscious of – / Unconscious of +
Spin down

Whereas a classical subjectively perceived object can spin in only one direction at a time—seemingly up and forward in time, or down and backward in time—a superposed quantum particle can be understood to be more objectively in two simultaneous "spin states"—both "spin up" and "spin down" at once—present.

A photon in superposition can be understood to be polarized in two different and conflicting directions simultaneously. And a quantum object can be understood to be both "there" and "not there" at the same time. In other words, objects in quantum superposition seem to not have certain definitive properties until the moment they are consciously measured, which some call *subjective experience.*

Entanglement allows two particles in superposition to forge an instant connection, so that an action performed on one of them (like measuring or perceiving one part of an entangled pair) affects both partners, even when they are separated by seemingly great distances. Entangled particles start out in a superposition of both up and down spin states. When an outside measurement on one member of the pair forces the particles to "pick" a single state, the two partners always pick coordinated states. This may be likened to the complementary pairs of opposite passionate behaviors—*feeling up and down*—lying within our super-posed human nature—inseparably entangled—*love*.

Chien-Shiung Wu's 1949 quantum experiment pro-vided early evidence of such entanglement, that is, pairs of photons from particle collisions remained polarized at right angles to each other—consistently—even when those photons were separated at a distance.

More and more brain scientists are identifying analo-gies between the above quantum phenomena and human perceptions and brain functions, episodic future imagina-tions and past memories, and the conscious and uncon-scious minds. So quantum processes are now considered to be part of cognitive, conscious and unconscious brain functions.

We now know from some biologists and scientists, and many other writers that our brains (EEGs) and hearts (ECGs) give off fields of intelligent information or intel-ligence that are picked up by other cells, which respond on a subtle, local and nonlocal level. We all share a field of interaction, so that when we think about someone with intentionality, we affect ourselves and them. These fields are scientifically demonstrable and reproducible today, so we know that they exist. We also know that these fields are electromagnetic and quantum in nature. Their influence is diminished over distance by the inverse square law and are undiminished over distance by nonlocal quantum entan-glement.

In 1993, theoretical astrophysicist Freeman J. Dyson, who won the prestigious Fermi Award, held that intelligence, and possibly consciousness, is a conserved subatomic yet universal field of charged particles of light, so our mind/body appears to be light-oriented—photoreceptive and photobroadcastive.

Consequently, the idea of being illuminated by the intelligent light of consciousness may not just be a metaphor; maybe it's actually more meaningful than first meets the eye. Maybe the whole universe is a matrix of intelligent light and its charged particles.

To me, to worship God means to recognize that mind and intelligence are woven into the fabric of our universe in a way that altogether surpasses our comprehension.
—FREEMAN J. DYSON

We have energetic light particles: photons. They're essentially massless, chargeless, timeless, and spaceless. The photon is, in essence, unconditioned. Light itself is likened to an imponderable spiritual essence that is not exactly touchable or measurable by itself. (Richard Feynman, the Nobel Prize winner, said that we don't really know what energy is.) The second you measure it, you convert it into something else. By itself, it's an imponderable essence that's spaceless, timeless, massless, and chargeless—in a sense, enlightened or intelligent energy and information, or what some ancient philosophers have called *spirit*.

Photon energy is the energy carried by a single photon. The amount of energy it carries is directly proportional to its electromagnetic frequency and thus, equivalently, is inversely proportional to the wavelength. The higher the photon's frequency, the shorter its wavelength and the higher its energy. Equivalently, the longer the photon's wavelength, the lower its frequency or energy. In relation to conscious awareness, this is likened to high-energy and -frequency simultaneous contrast of perception and low-energy and -frequency sequential contrast of perception.

In essence, these high energy and frequency particles of light can be decayed or broken down further into lower energy and frequency *positrons* and *electrons*. These possess characteristics—space, time, mass, and charge—they are existing conditional states of matter. So neutral energy can be converted into charged matter and matter into energy by Einstein's equation.

As a result, in similitude, an unconditional state of masterful enlightened consciousness can be converted or decayed into conditional states of mass full "endarkened" consciousness. According to the noted theoretical physicist John Wheeler, an unconditional state of full consciousness is love, or perfect divine love, according to Leibniz. Conditional states of mass consciousness are called *emotions*, which can be either positive or negative, where you are conscious of the positives and unconscious of the negatives, or conscious of the negatives and unconscious of the positives. The unconscious portion is where you are in the dark.

From a couple of unconditional photons, which are, again, in essence spaceless, timeless, massless, and charge-less, you can generate a pair of conditioned, complementary opposite particles—a positron and an electron—which express conditional characteristics of space, time, mass, and charge. The initial neutral photons are energy or spirit; the secondary charged particles are expressions of matter. In physics terms these are also called bosons and fermions, or force and source particles. The ancient Hermetic teaching said that vital or energetic spirit without matter is expressionless, and matter without spirit is motionless. Enlightening spirit represents unconditional love, while matter deals with conditional emotions—things that emotionally matter to you.

Love and Emotions

To view this in psychological terms, love—which I define as the synthesis and synchronicity of all complementary opposites—can be divided or polarized into complementary opposite emotions. Love is not just happiness; love is not just sadness; love is the synthesis and synchronicity of the two. Love is simultaneously both attraction and repulsion: "I like you"; "I dislike you"; "Come close to me"; "Get away from me." It's both sides simultaneously: attraction and repulsion. These two seemingly oscillating components make up love. Again, love is a synthesis and synchronicity of all complementary opposites—though most individuals are conscious of only one side of the love equation at once—the other side remaining unconscious.

Inside the central heart of your most integrated being—your medial prefrontal cortex, inside the physical and metaphorical heart—your intracardiac nerve network, you have a simultaneous receiving and broadcasting system of afferent and efferent nerves for maintaining a perfect brain and heart rhythm and a homeostatic healing state of unconditional love. That's why your brain and heart can synchronize and access a balanced state of love. All imbalanced or subjectively biased illusions are expressed throughout the rest of your body, where you have and experience conditioned and polarized emotional states.

Emotions are either positively or negatively charged. We'll call this positive charge *happiness* and this negative charge *sadness*: elation and depression, infatuation and resentment. If you see more positives than negatives or more negatives than positives, you have an emotion that moves you either impulsively towards or instinctively away, and you're attracted or repelled. In either case, the emotion is running you extrinsically, and you have an imbalanced state of brain and heart functions.

Let me take this one step further. As soon as your perception becomes lopsided and you no longer have a perfect synchronous synthesis of these two charged polarities, you automatically have an emotion that takes up space and time in your mind. That emotion runs you.

If you are infatuated with someone, they consume space and time in your mind; you can hardly get them out of your mind. Similarly with anger and resentment: you can be so resentful or angry with someone else that they consume space and time in your mind. In either case, you're no longer present, empowered, or inspired. You're distracted by the subjectively biased and polarized illusion you've deflected and projected onto the other individual.

They are now in a sense running you; you're disempowered, distracted, and disassociated.

The second you equilibrate that perception and see a perfect equilibrium between positives and negatives simultaneously, you are automatically liberated and reempowered, because the two in synthesis are spiritual power—vital energy—like a particle of light. As soon as you dissipate that synthesis and you fix it in polarized matter, you have energy in motion, and you yourself become dissipated by an emotion.

Most people think that love is happiness, kindness, and sweetness, but that does not prove true in reality. In fact, love consists of both nice and mean, kind and cruel, pleasant and unpleasant, "I like you" and "I dislike you," "Get out of my life" and "Come into my life." There's both attraction and repulsion, cooperation and competition, agreements and disagreements, peace and war. Although they appear to be separated sequentially in space and time, they are actually simultaneously present, but one side you are conscious of and the other side unconscious of.

Seeking a one-sided form of love is like trying to get a magnet with only one pole, which is impossible with a physical magnet. Emotionally, if you try to get rid of the negative and keep only the positive, you will oscillate between these two poles in a disordered, bipolar state, futilely attracted to the pleasure and avoiding the pain. What happens? You have a new set of pains.

It is unwise to try to separate the "inseparables," divide the "indivisibles," polarize the "unpolarizables," name the "ineffables,"or label the "unlabelables." The two sides in isolation are impostors.

The greater truth is that all events are neutral until somebody projects their value system onto them and subjectively labels them one way or the other. If it supports their value system, they call it good. If it challenges their value system, they call it bad. If they call it good and become highly infatuated with it, it runs them. If they call it bad and become highly resentful toward it, it runs them as well. In either case, they're disempowered by projecting their values onto externals. They're reempowered by equilibrating their perceptions synchronously. Now they are fully conscious of the whole, or enlightened and unattached.

Anything we're attracted to or repelled by runs our life. Anything we equilibrate, we run. We have a local influence on anything about which we have emotions, and we have a nonlocal influence on anything that we equilibrate.

As we've seen, the minimal unit of consciousness is a quantum. Any time we see half of a quantum—a positive or a negative—instead of the more objective, neutral whole, we're ignoring the other half, so we have an illusion and a lie about our subjective reality. That is ignorance. Ignorance is ignoring half of the quantum. It represents a state of division, conscious and unconscious, or awareness and unawareness or ignorance—endarkenment.

The truth is, there's nothing but love. All else is illusion. If we have an emotion about anything, we are incompletely aware and we're partly lying about the world or universe. We're seeing only half of it. The great American psychologist William James came to the same conclusion over a hundred years ago, and St. Augustine in his time said that the will of God was equilibrium—light: when the human will matches the will of God, the human state is attuned with the divine state—enlightened. When that occurs, you have humility before divinity and certainty before humanity. You realize that everything is in equilibrium; it's in order; you have a state of equanimity and equity. Nothing is missing—liberation and fulfillment.

Disease and Equilibrium

How can we have emotional equilibrium if we have lopsided perceptions? It's the old situation of garbage in, garbage out. If we perceive garbage on the outside, it's going to create garbage on the inside. Lopsided, disordered perceptions result in disordered emotional states of mind and body.

Furthermore, our peripheral motor responses are affected by our peripheral sensory perceptions via our central interneuron communications. If these sensory inputs are imbalanced, our motor output responses will be imbalanced. If our sensory input is distorted and does not see the full quantum awareness for what it is, but projects its own value systems and illusions onto the external world, it will automatically produce a disordered internal reaction physiologically, creating illness. Illness is the body's feedback mechanism to reveal to the conscious mind what it hasn't loved, or hasn't perceived both sides of simultaneously: the conscious and the unconscious.

Your body is doing all that it can to teach you how to love—how to be authentic and enlightened. It's giving you feedback in the form of symptoms in order to guide you and direct you back into equilibrium, where you perceive both sides of each event simultaneously. Whenever we have a disequilibrium in our perception and we are either impulsively infatuated or instinctively resentful—we are conscious of one side and unconscious of the other—this imbalance becomes stored in our subconscious mind irrespective of space or time. Some event can happen when we're five years old, and fifty-five years later, we can still have the resulting emotion running our lives. Until we equilibrate that emotion, we are in bondage to the incomplete perception. As soon as we equilibrate it, we're freed.

In his work in quantum physics, Erwin Schrödinger showed that before you open a box containing a cat and a radioactive material, the cat has the potential to be either alive or dead, but the second you open it and observe or measure it, it becomes either one or the other. Before you measure something, it's simply neutral and lives in a state of superposition, with the potential for both possibilities simultaneously. The second you measure it, or collapse the wave function, it has characteristics: alive or dead. As soon as we measure any event with our limited and illusive sensory perceptions, we tend to view it in a lopsided fashion, happy or sad, positive or negative, creating a split conscious and unconscious portion in our awareness. The ignored or unconscious portion holds the hidden variables to our full conscious or enlightened awareness.

If I walk on the street, become infatuated with somebody, and put them up on a pedestal, I will in turn minimize myself relative to them. If I become resentful and put them down into the pit, I will minimize that individual and put myself up. Anytime I put myself up or down relative to somebody else, I'm disempowered, because in either case, they represent the part that I'm not willing to own in myself. I am either too humble or too proud to own what I perceive in them. I am disempowered through disowning the unreflected parts that I perceive in them.

Every time we judge an individual or ourselves and put them or ourselves on a pedestal or in a pit, we exaggerate or minimize our perceptions and lie about our reality. And whenever we distort our reality or lie about anything, we generate a bipolar response. How can we have magnetism when we're trying to perceptually create only one pole of a magnet? Magnetism is produced by embracing both poles. If I desired to accumulate one-sided coins and I acquired the first coin, and all I wanted was the head instead of the tail, how many coins could I accumulate?

But if I embrace the heads and the tails simultaneously, and desire to accumulate two-sided coins, I can stack up a lot of coins.

It's the same with our true self-worth—which is the synthesis and synchronicity of our elevated and depressed self-esteems. Our true self-worth is directly proportional to the extent that we can simultaneously embrace the two sides of the events in our life and the two sides of our reactions to those events. The second we take an elevated or proud or a depressed or shamed stance, we become a victim of circumstance, because we're projecting our elusive values system onto an event and ourselves that are both actually neutral. Two people may see the same event completely differently according to their own projected values. The actual event is superposed or neutral until someone projects their subjectively biased interpretation onto it and labels it one-sidedly.

When you're stuck in the belief that any given individual, event, or yourself is unilaterally good or bad, or positive or negative, you become the victim of either your self-minimizing or self-aggrandizing response to this infatuation or resentment, and you become stuck in moral hypocrisy. But if you perceive others, events, and yourself as being essentially neutral, you liberate yourself from these false assumptions, emotions, and personas, and you awaken your more enlightened state.

When you can become conscious of what is unconscious in your awareness, you can become fully conscious. When you can become aware of the benefits of what you initially resented and the drawbacks to what you initially infatuated with, you can liberate yourself from your illusive or distortive emotions that run you, occupy space and time in your mind, and distract you.

Your response has little to do with what happens to you, but a lot to do with how you perceive it. I've taken over a hundred thousand people through a method that dissolves perceptions they have labeled traumatic from the past, neutralized them, and turned them into opportunities to soar. I know people that have had airplane crashes, been thrown out of cars, beaten, stabbed, hijacked, ransomed, or raped. No matter what the perceived trauma or tragedy, is, there's a way of turning it into a superimposed state of love again. There's a full quantum, more enlightened experience; finding it sets them free. The more down-and-out they've been, the greater their capacity is to move up and in, and the more powerful the transformational experience they can have.

I've worked with thousands of people who have had transformations in their health, but that was not necessarily the primary intention of working with them in that moment. I may have no intent of curing any so-called illness; I simply have the intent of equilibrating their imbalanced mind. In this process of returning them to a state of equanimity, the individual's physiology changes. (The ancient proverb "Take no credit; take no blame" is the essence of healing.) You can't be present as long as you're in the state of projecting blame or credit, because you're either resentful toward or infatuated with others; you're either building yourself up or beating yourself up with pride or shame, both of which result in distress-induced illness.

The transcendent function is a matter of being present with people and helping them be present with themselves. You won't be present as long as you are being run either by future imagined philias and phobias or by past remembered states of shame or pride.

Future imagined fear is an assumption that some event in the future will come in through your sensory perceptions that will involve more pain than pleasure, more loss than gain, more negative than positive. When you have guilt, which is the product of memory, you're assuming that you have caused more loss than gain, more negative than positive, more pain than pleasure, to yourself or somebody else in the past. Both of these responses are imbalanced perceptual illusions.

The Authentic Self

Let's try an experiment. Pick a time when somebody criticized you, put you down, ridiculed you, and supposedly hurt your feelings. Write this moment down. Isolate the place, the time, the individual, or the where, when, and who. Now identify exactly the same moment when somebody was praising you, lifting you up, or supporting you. Whether it was one or many, male or female, close or distant, virtual or real, who was lifting you, supporting you, and building you up at the simultaneous moment that somebody else was putting you down?

Each of your perceptions involves a contrast, a pair of opposites occurring simultaneously. To perceive one without the other leaves you either emotionally attracted or repelled and feeling disordered. To perceive both simultaneously leaves you feeling loved and ordered and reflects a higher degree of emotional intelligence.

In physiology circles, for every oxidation there is a reduction. In physics circles, for every positive there is a negative—a symmetrical conservation of charge. In sociological circles, for every position there is an opposition, according to the law of eristic escalation. In theological circles, it has been stated that the will of God is equilibrium. When your will or intention matches the divine will, the laws of the universe, you experience grace.

I'm going to make a statement that you're probably going to think is a bit wild: nobody is going to put you down without somebody else, real or virtual, simultaneously putting you up. You may be only initially conscious of one and initially unconscious of the other, but the other is actually present, to be intuitively realized once you are fully conscious.

Now do the opposite. Think of a time when somebody put you up on a pedestal and really praised and honored you. Locate the time and space and individual. Then identify who at the same moment came down on you. It could one or many, male or female, close or distant, virtual or real. In any event, both sides of the full event are occurring, because when somebody's putting you down and challenging you, in another way they're admiring you, thinking you're capable of handling their criticism. When somebody's supporting you, in a sense they're saying you're not capable of achieving on your own. Both sides of the quantum equation are occurring simultaneously, but you are probably only conscious of one side at a time unless you ask the intuitive question that unveils the accompanying unconscious side. This is the key to awakening a greater emotional intelligence.

Like a magnet, with its two pole,s each event has both poles or sides. You won't have one side without the other. A loving synthesis and synchronicity of complementary opposites is occurring at each moment of perception, but people tend to become conscious of one side and ignore or become unconscious of the other. The emotion resulting from this one-sided illusion is then stored in your subconscious mind and becomes gravitational baggage that ages. At this point, you go into a time-full mind and age-full body instead of timeless mind and ageless body state. The second you're aware of the synchronicity, you have an enlightened, timeless, eternal mind, and you have no aging. You only age when you experience the arrow of time and have past memories and future imaginations, when you're lopsided in your perceptions, and you have disorder or missing information in your perceptual state. An enlightening photon does not age. To the photon, its departure and arrival occurs at the same time.

Your present, timeless mind emerges the moment you perceive both sides of an event or an individual synchronously—the moment your perceptual equation becomes perfectly and simultaneously balanced. It thus differs from a "timeful," "time-filled," or diachronic mind, which is living through time; synchronous mind is dissolving time. It is acausal. Dissolving time means simultaneously seeing both sides at the same moment and realizing there's nothing but full quantum enlightened love.

Expressing your authentic self occurs when you are neither exaggerating nor minimizing yourself or others. Let me go further into how you can become more balanced and neutral and express your most authentic and enlightened self.

When you exaggerate others and put them on pedestals, you will tend to minimize yourself through comparison or contrast.

Rather than being your authentic self, at various moments in your life, I'm sure you have met individuals that you looked up to, admired, were drawn to, and maybe even have tried to imitate. You may have put them above you and seen them as greater than you, or more skilled in some capacity—possibly more intelligent, more viable in business, wealthier, more stable in relationships, more socially connected, possibly more physically fit and attractive, or even more spiritually aware. If so, you have most likely to have exaggerated them and minimized yourself.

When you overvalue others, you tend to devalue yourself.

When you exaggerate others, you are also minimizing their downsides.

When you look up to somebody and think they are greater than you, you tend to exaggerate what you perceive to be their "good" qualities and downplay any of their perceived downsides or "bad" activities or qualities. In other words, you tend to exaggerate how great they are. In doing so, you tend to become conscious of their upsides and unconscious of their downsides, while in turn becoming conscious of your own downsides and unconscious of your upsides, relatively speaking.

This subjectively distorted assessment will lead you to become too humble to admit that what you see in them is also inside of you to the same degree. This often leads to intimidation, difficulty in speaking, and lowered self-esteem and self-confidence.

When you exaggerate others, you can devalue yourself and inject their values into your life.

The moment you look up to somebody and minimize yourself, you devalue yourself. You disown their admired traits in yourself, so that you play small. You are also likely to inject their values into your life, and even envy them. This can also cloud the clarity of your own highest value, or meaningful purpose in life and distract you.

The Green-Eyed Monster

Envy, aka the green-eyed monster, is assuming or perceiving that someone has something that you don't have. It could be their level of intelligence, achievement, wealth, relationships, prestige, appearance, or spiritual awareness.

Let's say you want a promotion at work, but somebody else comes in and takes the position. You will probably feel envious of that employee for getting that position. You might also resent the supervisor who made the hiring decision.

If you are a woman who is dating someone and another woman comes along who has a more "intelligent" conversation with your partner, you may also come across the green-eyed monster. You might envy that woman for having the intelligence to relate to your partner in a way that you seemingly cannot. Her ability to communicate with your partner might be the source of your envy. This could lead to further jealousy: you could fear that this woman will take your partner.

But as Ralph Waldo Emerson said, "Envy is ignorance, imitation is suicide."

To think that someone has something more than you—for instance more money or more business viability—is to be ignorant of the form of genuine wealth or achievement you actually already have.

Within this dynamics of resentment lies a hidden gem. You have within you the potential to awaken to your own inner power and influence.

When the green-eyed monster creeps in and you feel envy and jealousy, it could serve as an eye-opener and catalyst to empower yourself.

If you're disempowered, assuming that another individual has something you don't, you're vulnerable. The bigger the discrepancy between what you think they have and what you don't think you have, the more vulnerable you will be. Feelings of envy and jealousy are partly byproducts of not empowering yourself, or not recognizing the power you already have.

Instead of being envious of someone, it is wiser to go and discover how you do have it in your own form, thereby empowering yourself.

Identify what exactly you perceive the other individual to have that you assume you don't have, and see how you actually do have this in your own unique form—according to you own unique hierarchy of values.

For instance, if you perceive someone to have more wealth or money than you, discover where you presently have an equivalent form of genuine wealth, which, if repackaged and sold to interested parties, could be converted into money, financial assets, or wealth.

You might have it partly in intellectual property that could be worth millions.

You might have it partly in intrinsically valued business assets that could be worth millions.

You might have it partly in financial assets already worth millions.

You might have it partly in your stable family relationship dynamic that could be worth millions. If you had to put a price on your relationship or your children, you might reckon it in the millions.

You might have it partly in leverageable social networking contacts that could be worth millions.

You might have it partly in your physical appeal or attractiveness that could be worth millions.

You might have it in inspirational or spiritual wisdom or assets that could be worth millions.

Once you become aware of your currently hidden and convertible assets and discover you already have the same traits or even equivalent possessions as the one you envy, you will realize nothing is truly missing within you and you will empower yourself. It was simply in another stored form in accordance with your higher set of values.

It is wise to empower yourself in all the seven major areas of life:

- Spiritual awareness
- Mental understanding and wisdom
- Social power and leadership
- Familial love, relationships, and intimacy
- Physical health and well-being
- Financial independence and freedom
- Vocational service and achievement

To level the playing field, just keep digging into your unconscious mind, discover your hidden assets, and begin consciously empowering all seven areas of your life. The more you own your own power, the less time you will spend with the green-eyed monster due to the law of contrast and comparison.

At the higher, more expanded, or universal level of your most authentic self, or at the level of what theologians call your enlightened soul, nothing is missing; there is total fullness, fulfillment, or *pleroma*, as the ancient Christian Gnostics called it. Or as Empedocles once described it, all the four elements fire, air, water, earth, are united and integrated into the fifth, more universal filling element, aether, the quintessential (quintessence) of being—love.

At the lower, more narrowed, or fundamental level of your inauthentic self, your illusive senses, things appear to be missing, which the Gnostics called *kenoma*, or emptiness and void. What appears to be missing is whatever you are too humble or too proud to admit you have or that you admire or despise and judge in others.

What appears to be missing are all the parts you are unconscious of and have disowned from not introspectively reflecting, masterfully governing, or balancing your perceptions. When you begin to consciously own what you have disowned, you become more equitable, empowered, enlightened, and clear. And when you realize nothing is actually missing you begin to value you. When you value you, so does the world. The greater your true self-worth the greater is your contribution or offer to the world.

The more clearly you communicate what you can offer, the more you will receive what you desire.

Again, when you elevate someone else and minimize yourself, you are not being your authentic self.

No human being can endure living in other people's values. It's futile and unsustainable. Like every individual, you live by a set of priorities, a set of values that is unique to you. Whatever is highest on your list of values, you spontaneously are inspired to do. And whenever you have injected the values of others you admire into yourself, those values compete with your own highest values and create an internal conflict, which results in uncertainties and often repression. Instead of living as you truly are, you are attempting to live as you think you should or hope be.

It is wise to recognize the uncertainty that you will feel when you minimize yourself as normal biological feedback: it is letting you know that you are attempting to *not* be your authentic self. Whenever you are giving yourself internal imperatives—"I should," "I ought to," "I have to," or "I must," try to see these statements as feedback telling you that you are futilely attempting to live in other elevated or admired people's values instead of your own.

When you exaggerate others and minimize *you*, you are likely to diminish yourself and play smaller than you are. This can result in a form of inner dysmorphia. Some people have an internalized body dysmorphia, unable to see the magnificence of their body when they compare themselves to attractive and admired others. You can also have a similar internalized dysmorphia in your intellectual pursuits, your business, finances, family, relationships, social life, physical health, and even your spiritual life.

We are not here to put people on pedestals or in pits; we are also here to put them in our hearts. We are also here to have reflective awareness—the highest level of awareness we can have—where we perceive both sides of them simultaneously and love them. Which helps us see both sides of ourselves and love us.

When you minimize others, you tend to exaggerate yourself. When you exaggerate yourself, you also tend to minimize others. You are also likely to resent them, withdraw from, and want to avoid them. In the process of exaggerating yourself and minimizing them, you tend to become conscious of your own upsides and unconscious of your downsides. As a result, you might become proud and self-righteous and look down on them.

When you exaggerate yourself, you are not being authentic.

When you exaggerate yourself, you are likely to project your values onto others.

Values in society tend to go or flow from those who have the most power, perceptually, to those that have least power. So when you exaggerate yourself, you are more likely to project your values onto others and futilely expect them to live in your values.

For example, you might find yourself saying, "you should," "you ought to," "you're supposed to," "you've got to," "you have to," "you must," or "you need to."

You might find yourself feeling frustrated because they aren't doing what you think they are "supposed" to do.

Your true self-worth occurs when you have reflective awareness, are objective and authentic, and don't inject or project values.

Neither narcissism nor altruism by themselves are sustainable. True self-worth occurs when you have equanimity within yourself and equity between yourself and others, when you have reflective awareness, and when you are not too proud or too humble to admit that what you see in others is inside your whole authentic self. Welcome to a heightened emotional intelligence state.

In other words, when you are in a state of objectivity and neutrality, you don't fear the loss of that which you seek. Nor do you fear the gain of that which you try to avoid. Here you are most authentic and empowered. Here you have a superposition of both sides simultaneously. You are self-actualized and self-governed.

Striving for that which is unavailable and trying to avoid that which is unavoidable is the source of human suffering. So, any time you are inauthentic, you are likely to go into "suffering" mode, which is essentially feedback to let you know that you're not being your inspired, enlightened, and authentic self.

Your physiology, psychology, sociology, and theology are all designed as homeostatic negative feedback systems to bring you back into authenticity.

When you are reflective and can own the traits or behaviors you see in others equally, you are able to obtain your authentic and essential self, your enlightened soul. Your soul is the unjudging state of unconditional love.

This reflective state is where you are most objective and inspired, where you tend to live congruently by your highest values, and when you are the most spontaneously active. It's also when you are most integrated embracing both your "hero" and "villain" sides instead of denying any of them, because you have recognized there is nothing missing within you and nothing to get rid of or acquire. You don't need to get rid of one half of yourself to love your authentic self.

When you see someone displaying or demonstrating traits, actions, or inactions that you despise or resent, it is wise to self-reflect and identify where you have displayed or demonstrated those same traits, actions, or inactions to the same degree, quantitatively and qualitatively.

Ask yourself what were the upsides, benefits, or advantages of their behavior. In doing so, you will help bring your mind into balance and see both sides of each event simultaneously.

All events and actions are neutral until you judge them with a skewed, subjective bias. It is wise to ask questions to equilibrate and liberate your mind, because you can't have a balanced physiology without a balanced psychology. This more neutral state reflects a higher emotional intelligence.

Your actions are a byproduct of your perceptions. When you balance your perceptions, you are likely to have more moderate or governed actions. If not, you might find yourself with extreme volatilities and perturbations in your perceptions and ungoverned emotional reactions.

So the moment you own the traits, actions, or inactions, neutralize them, go to the moments where and when you have also displayed or demonstrated them, and then find the upsides or downsides of each of them and balanced them all out, you will in turn dissolve your inauthentic personas that take the form of pride and shame.

When you dissolve your pride, shame, infatuation, and resentment, you are more able to access your authentic self.

You also dissolve the subjectively biased labels on your authentic self or others resulting from the rigidity of your misperceptions of your inauthentic self or others and allow you and them to be just human beings with your and their own unique set of values. You are more likely to realize that there is no reason to judge them, and no reason to judge yourself.

You are not here to compare yourself to others. You are here to compare your daily actions to your own dreams, and to your own highest priorities or values.

Love as Balance

If we define love as a synthesis and synchronicity of all complementary opposites, or a simultaneous balance of positive and negative perceptions and their corresponding emotions, we can see that the purpose of marriage is not a one-sided hedonistic happiness; the purpose of marriage is equilibration, love, and authenticity. If you come home cocky and elated, the one you love will pop that pimple and bring you back down into authenticity. If you're down, thinking you're worth less than what is true, they're there with a shovel lifting you up, again bringing you back up to a state of authenticity. The same is true for your employees and your children. Your children are genetic expressions of an equating force: whatever you disown, whatever you repress, whatever you swear you would never do, they will manifest and specialize in it, to humble your judgment. They'll live out what you repress in order to teach you how to equilibrate and love the part you're disowning. Whatever you keep running away, avoid, or repress you will keep running into or breed.

Now try this process another way. Think of a time when you ridiculed or criticized somebody else. Then see who was there to lift them up and praise them—again one or many, male or female, real or virtual. You could not throw this process out of balance with all your intent. Even if you had the vilest and most negative intent, somebody else was equilibrating it. You won't be able to override this law, which overrides the will of any human individual. This is not a thinking exercise. It is an intuitive one. The more present you are at the moment of perception, the more spontaneously the answer will emerge to balance the equation.

Now do the opposite: think of a time when you praised somebody. Who else was slamming them? Or whom did you get really close to but was rejected by somebody else as a result? Maybe you befriended someone and made someone else jealous of them. It will be real or virtual in their minds. When you are aware of both sides simultaneously, your emotional intelligence is high.

It is at the moment of perception that your conscious and unconscious minds split. And it is at the moment of perception that you can actually synchronously rejoin them and become fully conscious of both sides simultaneously, like the enlightening superposition of particle and antiparticle. The synthesis and synchronicity or superposition of praise and reprimand, pleasure and pain, support and challenge is what makes up true mindful, unconditional love.

What would happen if you realized that each of your perceptions has two sides or poles like the previously described magnet. And one side does not come without the other? The two sides are actually inseparable, but your subjectively biased subcortical brain, or amygdala-centered animal mind, has filtered out half of the equation, making you blind and ignorant by adding valency to your perceptions.

Your sensory perception works through contrast so you won't consciously experience a pain without a corresponding unconscious pleasure; so too, you won't cause a pain without causing a corresponding pleasure, though someone else may bias their perception. Your mind may become conscious of one side and unconscious of the other and swear that one exists without the other, but your higher brain/mind simultaneously and objectively perceives through contrasts and contains the whole. It is like a particle and an antiparticle, or memory and antimemory, being synthesized and synchronized into an unconditional and enlightened love.

Most people are wandering around dissociatedly, assuming that external events are happening to them. They live with false attribution biases and causalities and giving credit or blame. They're projecting their value systems on the exterior world and expecting the world to match their unrealistic expectations. If some event or object doesn't support their value system, they think it's terrible. They don't take the time to look for the equal and opposite and discover the yin inside the yang or the yang inside the yin. (As Newton said, every action has an equal and opposite reaction.) They don't take the time to look for this opposite equal, so they become victims of their own incomplete perception. Because they have taken a stance, they have become victims of circumstance instead of playing in the dance. Playing in the dance is seeing the synthesis or both sides simultaneously or synchronously. Not perceiving simultaneously the pair of opposites, but perceiving sequentially the contrasting opposites, sometimes termed the diachronic state, an emotional state that disempowers you and puts you in bondage: you are now stuck in a polarized emotion because you've allowed yourself to believe an incomplete awareness or a lie about what actually has occurred, which is a state of endarkened mindlessness.

Prudence versus Decision

We can apply these insights to decision-making, of which there are two types: I'm going to call one *prudence* and the other *decision*. With decision, which means *to cut off* or *kill* a side, you have a duality of choices: you accept one and refuse—bring about the death of—the other. Hence decision is seeking something and avoiding something else, or its opposite. It is a choice made from pleasure and pain, seeking and avoidance, or bringing life to it and bringing death to it.

By contrast, prudence and wisdom arise from the more objectively balanced calling of the heart rather than the more subjectively imbalanced reactions due to more polarized sensory illusions. When you act from the heart, you act in love. When you react from the remaining body, you react with a polarized, attractive, or repulsive emotion. Emotional reactions are easy to make: you impulsively seek this and instinctively avoid that. But once you've done that, you realize what you thought would bring you pleasure has some pain to it and what you have avoided that you thought would be only painful had some pleasure to it.

Pleasure and pain are conserved in time and space. People get a new house and think, "I'll be happy now." No. All emotions are transient. They oscillate. Only love is eternal. Love, a synthesis and synchronicity of complementary opposites, is eternal; it never goes away, except perceptually. No human being has the power to interfere with the enlightening and fulfilling divine order called love. The greater your emotional intelligence the greater your gratitude, certainty, presence and love.

Here is another aspect of this situation: You may be dwelling on some so-called terrible past event, and somebody comes along saying, "Yeah, but let's go forward. Think about your goals." Another version: you're dwelling about your fantasies for the future, and somebody pulls you back, saying, "Remember when you did or experienced this nightmarish action in the past?" Still another: you dwell on how magnificent it was when you were a teenager, but somebody tells you, "Yeah, but if you don't do something different with your life, Lord knows where you're going to go." Now you're down. Not only do you simultaneously attract an equal and opposite event in emotional charge, you also attract an equal and opposite charged event in time. It is similar to temporal entanglement in quantum physics.

This I call the *quadrant of emotions.*

If you are at home talking about the good or bad days coming in the future, your spouse will point out the bad or good old days of the past. If you are at home talking about the good or bad old days of the past, your spouse will point out the bad or good new days of the future. Your family dynamics help you and all of your family members remain present in time.

You also won't go into your future imagination without simultaneously going into your past memory. Besides having every imagination composed of content from your memory and having every memory composed of content from your imagination, both are malleable and can be distorted. Reading William James' writings when I was age twenty-one gave me an insight into this dynamic: he said that memory doesn't exist without imagination, nor does imagination exist without memory. These two temporary mental storage depositories are actually keeping your emotional charges neutral and your spatial and temporal perceptions balanced in the present.

Your memory provides the building blocks for things you imagine. Your memories of things that have happened before also provide the building blocks of imagining possible futures. Memory is certainly critical for imagination.

Your imagination provides the building blocks for things you remember. Your imaginations of things that may happen after also provide the building blocks of remembered possible pasts. Imagination is certainly critical for memory.

By age twenty-three, I discovered clinically that episodic memories simultaneously had episodic imaginations, like the conscious and unconscious portions of the mind. Later, in 2018, neuroscience revealed their inseparability. Your brain maintains the present moment by integrating the past with the future. It also maintains homeostasis by integrating positive and negative facilitation and inhibition, or depolarizations and hyperpolarizations.

Your integrative brain/mind will not let you get out of the present by going into fantasies or nightmares of the future without equilibrating them through their opposite nightmares or fantasies in the past. Your forebrain/mind, with its intuition, keeps you equilibrated. There's an ordered field of intelligence that equilibrates you both in time and in emotional charge. In actuality, there's nothing but love and the enlightened full quantum state or mindfulness. Your brain/mind is capable of awakening up to this full quantum twenty-four hours a day, but it is caught by your subcortical brain's subjectively biased sensory illusions that it projects onto objects and events stemming from your value systems. Let's look further into value systems.

2

The Power of Polarities

Your set of priorities or values has much to do with what you perceive to be missing in your life. Let's say you perceive that you have no relationship, or certain parts of your relationship appears to be missing—the parts you are infatuated with, or fantasize about; you look for a relationship to fulfill what you perceive to be absent, don't you? If you perceive that you have insufficient money, you look for ways and means to earn more income. If you perceive that you have insufficient numbers of clients, you look for ways to acquire more clients. Hence *your perceived voids drive your set of values*. Whatever you perceive as most missing becomes most important.

Imagine going to a bank and saying, "I'd like to receive a $100,000 loan, but I have a sketchy business plan and no collateral." The bank loan officers probably won't lend their money to you until you come up with a more probable and detailed plan and/or $100,000 of collateral. The world around you reflects and provides you with whatever you have that is equivalent and don't currently deny. If you act on the assumption that you have a lack of money, or the lack of a means to earn it, you are going to keep deterring others from probably wanting to give you any money. This is partly due to your self-perception and economically non-equivalent provisions. You're coming from an assumption that it's missing and the world around you is reflecting this.

The truth is, you are not actually missing an equivalent form of genuine wealth. It is already potentially there in one or many of the other forms—intellectual property, business opportunities and leads, family influence, support and stability or children, social contacts and leverage, physical attractiveness or beauty, or spiritual awareness and service. But you may not often recognize, acknowledge, or honor it in these other forms because you do not fully know your true value systems, which underly them. You're probably infatuated with a certain object or outcome, but you think it's not currently there in your life, but its equivalent actually is, although in a form that matches your true hierarchy of values, and you are expecting it to be in the form that aligns with someone else's value system that you admire. As a result, you keep seeking it in their form while not acknowledging it in its present form. As soon as you realize it's actually there and present, but in a form that's different from the one you imagined or fantasized about, you finally realize you already have it, but it is in the form that aligns with your true set of values. This state of abundance allows you to go to the bank of life and receive it in the new form. Change your values and you change its form. Once you realize that it is not missing, you can convert it from the form it is currently in to the one desired, and you will no longer feel as desperate, but instead more abundant.

Your fulfillment emerges the moment you honor your own set of values and set your expectations to align with them or transform your set of values to match the forms you seek.

Define exactly what you think you've lost. Identify it specifically in all its details, asking, what form is it in now? Find the equivalent form it's actually in; don't stop until you do. It can be one or many forms in the seven areas of your life. The second you realize it's there, you no longer feel lack. When you no longer feel lack, you're no longer run by extrinsic voids and values that are the source of your polarized emotions and pushing your buttons. The more you feel fulfilled, the greater your emotional intelligence.

Motivation versus Inspiration

There's a difference between extrinsic motivation and intrinsic motivation, or inspiration: a calling from within. The first comes from an illusion generated from the exterior; the second comes from the heart and most authentic self or soul. Most people are living quiet lives of desperation. They're attempting to live by somebody else's value system without realizing that the system of values they are attempting to conform to isn't even theirs in the first place. They believe there's something missing and feeling empty inside because they're buying into a mythical idea of the way it's supposed to be according to the herd, the tradition, the convention, derived from outer authorities.

My observation, definition, and origin of clinical depression is a comparison of your current perceived reality with an unrealistic expectation, fantasy, delusion, or myth about how you believe or think it's supposed to, should be, or wish it would be. But what you think is supposed to be is often not even realistic. If you say, "I want a happy relationship with someone who's nice to me all the time," you're unrealistically expecting an illusion and almost guaranteed to attract somebody who challenges you or beats you up, because you're living in a fantasy, and the disowned part will draw in someone who balances it out to make sure you are authentic and grow.

When you seek out or are addicted to one-sided, supportive fantasies, you become juvenile, dependent on that which you impulsively seek. You require its very opposite polarity to break your addiction and to help you grow up and become more preciously independent. Maximum growth and development occurs at the border between support and challenge, ease and difficulty, cooperation and competition, peace and war, prey and predator, parasympathetic and sympathetic function.

If you attempt to treat someone for clinical depression of this nature, you're partly wasting your time until you can find out their fantasy and break it open and ground or neutralize it. I once worked with a client diagnosed with schizophrenia who had a complete fantasy that he was above all students, all teachers, all people at school; therefore he was not applying effort and was failing in school.

Close loved ones were trying to extrinsically motivate him, but without results. I spent almost two hours dissolving this gentleman's unrealistic fantasy about himself and his role amongst others. Then I had him identify his highest values: what was most missing and most important in his life by having him complete the Demartini Value Determination Process (which I have available for free on my website: www.drdemartini.com). I found out the form of what he thought was missing was and then I associated his educational classes with the highest of his values.

All of a sudden he came into an integrated state for a moment. After he became integrated I talked to his parents, who said, "What happened to our son? He's a different boy."

Today psychiatry is sometimes applying what some call barbaric treatments on schizophrenic clients because it is predominantly pharmaceutically and electronically minded more than cognitively minded. Some psychiatrists don't focus on values and psychodynamics; some psychologists do but predominantly from a victim, moral ideal, disease label model; they don't frequently or initially understand that there's a full quantum simultaneously and contrastingly occurring in their clients' brains/minds. Once these clients become aware of both polarities simultaneously, their brain undergoes neuroplastic changes.

Your forebrain/mind is self-governing and homeostatic and has many negative feedback loops and entangled synchronicities functioning within it. It is attempting to reveal that there is nothing but a balanced love; all else is a subjectively biased illusion. If you come from the perspective that there's anything but love, you're already in a paradigm that's going to keep you caught in a cycle of false attribution biases, judgments, and false causalities.

No therapy can ever be complete until the assumed causes equal effects in space-time. Let's say that some woman yells at me. And I perceive that what she stated hurt; I think she did this to me: she's the cause, and I'm the effect. Then I run to my therapist saying, "She's the bad one. I'm the innocent one, the victim." If the therapist supports that myth, it will keep me in therapy for as long as I remain in that myth.

My perception has little to do with that individual, but it has much to do with my expectations, myths about human behavior, and the impulsive and instinctive reactions emerging out of previously stored emotional baggage in my subconscious mind. Instead, I could say, "Let's find out where I have displayed or demonstrated the same equivalent behavior and then find out the many benefits it actually simultaneously provided. Let me stack them up and find out how they link to and serve my highest values. How is this serving me?" I can also find out who is doing the opposite to me at the same time. Once I acknowledge that this behavior is a mirror reflection of my disowned parts, I can thank that individual for waking me up. Now I'm out of therapy. My emotional intelligence has inwardly asked me more resourceful questions and set me free.

Even if someone is acting in a way that I highly resent, it is my perception, decision, and action or reaction to their behavior that I have governance over, not so much their behavior. It is wise to own what you judge in others through reflection. It is wise to also own the reality of why you are having the response you have. This individual isn't doing this out of the blue. There's some dynamic going on in a subtle level between you two.

How many times have you had moments of inner peace and calm followed by moments of inner turmoil? For many years, in my socially misinformed ignorance, I used to strive for one-sided peace. Now I realize that this is not what we're here for, because we get both sides: cooperation and competition, peace and war, nice and mean, kind and cruel, support and challenge. The order and chaos both serve us; we need them both in order to grow. That is why our physical body has the parasympathetic and sympathetic nervous system portions and responses. The people that challenge us make us precociously independent. The people that support us can help make us juvenile and dependent. We need both synchronously to maximize our potential as human beings. I'm not here to promote one side or the other, because both of them are illusions. Both are required for maximum growth and development and for maximum resilience and adaptability.

Notice how this dynamic plays out in world events. Throughout history, the boundaries of many if not most nations have changed. No nation is designed to be stagnant; it's constantly changing. Notice too how in some cases, the people that are trying to promote peace are the ones at war with another group. Some of my students have been involved in teaching the delegates of the United Nations. In this process, they've come to realize that these idealisms don't have any permanent reality. The reality is that people are individuals, with both polarities, just like everyone else. I can be as nice as a pussycat or as mean as a tiger, depending upon whether I perceive you to support or challenge my hierarchy of values, and so can you. But my level of emotional intelligence will determine to what extreme.

Family Dynamics

Would you agree that at times you're both kind and cruel according to your own or somebody else's perception? It may not be your intent, but that's the reality. If you get married, you still have the same situation. You don't get peace alone. The purpose of marriage isn't to bring peace or happiness; the purpose of it is to equilibrate any disowned parts and love them for the sake of becoming authentic and whole. Each marriage will have agreements and disagreements, attractions and repulsions, and possibly even hugs and grudges.

A lot of self-help relationship gurus are teaching and promoting little fantasy worlds and making you feel that you're supposed to and always going to be happy. In reality, that doesn't exist. What is real is balancing out your state.

Let's say that you have children. What happens then? Do you get more peace, or both calm and turmoil, peace and war? Say a family is driving in a car. The mother and father are in the front, and the children are in the back, fighting and screaming. The parents are trying to keep calm and say, "Johnny, would you please be quiet back there? Leave your brother alone."

A few minutes later, they're fighting again. Finally, the mother looks back and says, "Johnny, I told you to leave your brother alone. Sit back in your seat." Not long afterward, the two brothers are fighting again. The mother says, "All right, now you sit over here, and you sit over there, and you leave each other alone."

All this time, the father is trying to drive. Finally, he loses his calm, pulls over and starts screaming and yelling. Now the parents in front are temporarily at war from his overreaction and the children are temporarily peaceful. When the parents start to calm down, the children come back and start war again.

In a family dynamic, peace and war, the valences of charge, the positives and negatives, the pains and pleasures are conserved through time and space. Let's wake up to that greater truth. They are both of value, because somebody's bringing the support while somebody else is giving the challenge. This is the great law: somebody's supporting and somebody's challenging. That's the definition of love: peace and war, positive and negative, support and challenge. That is what love is, and it is what surrounds you. Again, love is the synthesis and synchronicity of all complementary opposites. When you're looking for full-time, one-sided love, you'll look for eternity and not find it. When you embrace the true and balanced form of love that surrounds you, it cannot escape you.

I've already suggested that you think of a time when somebody brought you down while somebody else was building you up. Now what if you went and you carried this process through all the way back to the earliest time in your life you can remember? Say you went back and identified every moment when somebody praised you and somebody else synchronously reprimanded you, and vice versa. Then look back at every moment when you praised someone but somebody else synchronously reprimanded them. If you did that for a thousand different situations, you would find that each one balanced itself out. Our subjective biases filter out from our full conscious awareness our unconscious blindness of the other side of the equation that makes up the whole truth of love.

If you realized that great truth, you'd have access to love in every moment of perception. You'd realize that the wisdom of your body and brain maintains this homeostatic state, but your subjective bias most often ignores it. You'd realize that there's an intelligence in the universe and in each of us making sure there's nothing but love, and all else is a subjective perceptual illusion. In this process, you would also realize that everything is a reflection of you, and anyone's behavior you don't love externally is a representation of the parts inside you haven't loved. It's just giving you an opportunity to love. Love is the synthesis and synchronicity of all complementary opposites. The height of emotional intelligence is this full conscious awareness.

Self-Image and Abuse

There is an equal amount of cooperation and competition, support and challenge, peace and war, friendliness and aggression in the world. The Global Peace Index

(GPI), a report produced by the Institute for Economics & Peace (IEP), measures the relative position of nations' and regions' peacefulness. The GPI ranks 163 independent states and territories (collectively accounting for 99.7 per cent of the world's population) according to their levels of peacefulness. Although there are slight fluctuations year to year, overall the peace and war ratios maintain relative equilibrium. The same was found within smaller social units, including families and each of us as individuals.

When local representatives from the Red Cross asked me to speak in Madrid, Spain, I learned that 75 percent of the women there are treated aggressively and often beaten by their husbands. Yet when I had the opportunity to work with the women there in 2003, the women in the group I was presented with were beating themselves up on the inside even more than their husbands were on the outside. Their own self-image was being depreciated, mainly because of their cultural religious idealism: they've had the fantasy of chaste ideals about how they're supposed to be living that were in conflict with their own ideals and their husband's demands. They were not living up to these fantasies, so they felt they were not good enough and not worthy. Furthermore, the injected religious value systems they were attempting to subordinate, encouraged these women not to work and become further educated; they were only "supposed to" be raising their families. These women were partly disempowered and dependent, and many of them inwardly resented it. In this process, the one who is the doormat is walked all over. Any area of your life you don't empower becomes an area others overpower.

These women were beating themselves up inwardly as much as those who are beating them outwardly, because they had some part of themselves that they felt was unworthy of love. They were subordinating to and trapped by social and religious moral hypocrisies. Moreover, the women who were being beaten were not knowing how to effectively communicate in terms of their husband's values. Finally, most of them feared being beaten and were almost addicted to the fantasy of a one-sided peace, support, and kindness. I found those three qualities in most of the cases. They were walking around with their philic fantasy and phobic fear, and whatever you fear is going to come near, because it's your fear, not others'.

Those addicted to peace often attract war.

Those addicted to protection often attract aggression.

The law of complementary opposites overrules local idealisms.

You may wonder how this principle may apply to small children. If you regress children back, you'll find out that many of them don't feel they deserve to be here. Many thought they should have been of the opposite sex; they shouldn't have been born this way; they're not worthy. As long as they have this internal perception, they attract events to wake them up, to say, "You are worth something." No matter what we've done or not done, we're worthy of love, but sometimes children hold on to misperceptions and concerns inside their own consciousness and are not loving various aspects about themselves. We attract people who point that internal judgment or void out to us. Injury often means jury from within.

You may think these people are naive and innocent, but I've worked with women and children on the parts of themselves that they haven't loved and their thoughts that they are somehow not worthy of love. We dissolve those illusions, and the internal and external beating stops. Again, outer injury has its roots from the jury within. When the women in Spain dissolved their internal conflicts and self-depreciating illusions that they were somehow unworthy of love, and replaced them with more realistic objectives for themselves, and communicated their highest values in terms of their husbands', their husbands' aggressive behavior changed. We have the ability to influence the dynamic around us nonlocally once we influence the dynamic within us. Once we comprehend the hidden order within and become authentic, the outer chaos attempting to make us authentic subsides.

I once had a woman come to my signature seminar program The Breakthrough Experience. She was in the process of putting a restraining order on her husband. He was beating her regularly, and she was actually nearly at gunpoint a couple of times. The guy was about to be restrained or possibly go to jail. This woman had all the socially legitimate reasons for blame. She was also highly supported and protected simultaneously by other wounded women.

At the Breakthrough Experience, she applied the Demartini Method on her husband, and guess what we found out? She was divorced from a previous marriage, had an illegitimate daughter from another man, and felt guilty about it. She had had an abortion when she was younger. She had some religious ideal of how she was supposed to be and didn't live up to that ideal experience, so she was shamefully inflicting anger upon herself. Then she lied to the next man she married, saying that she was somebody she really wasn't: she didn't want to have to live with her daughter in a rough area of town, and this man lived far out of that area and was financially stable. She got married to him under false pretenses, but didn't feel worthy of being with him. He was beating her up partly because she was beating herself up. She admitted she often provoked his anger knowingly.

I applied the Demartini Method with her, dissolved many of those self-depreciating illusions and self-judgments methodically, and found out where her inner worth was. I spent four or five hours with this woman finding out where she was beating herself up. She was beating her daughter up sometimes and she was beating up society, because it didn't match her ideal. When she finally equilibrated this perception, she calmed down. She had a catharsis, realizing that she was worthy of love for who she was once we put dozens of synchronously balancing puzzle pieces together. Her anger at herself and her situation and husband dissolved away.

When she completed the method, she felt appreciation and love. I said, "You can end up getting beaten by anybody when you go against them or highly challenge their highest values. So it is wise to clearly identify your husband's highest values and begin communicating what you would love in terms of these. If you keep going against them, he's going to treat you cruelly."

Each individual has a set or hierarchy of values. When you communicate in and support their highest values, they treat you nicely; they become more passive and give you freedom. The second you challenge these values, they become more aggressive, treat you cruelly, and give you constraint. How many times have you been nice or mean depending on whether somebody supports or challenges your highest values? Coming to realize your true whole and balanced nature and setting more realistic and balanced expectations is part of awakening your emotional intelligence.

In the case of this woman, we identified the husband's values, and I taught her how to communicate with care. The definition of *caring* is learning how to communicate your highest values in terms of the other's highest values. This is not the same as being *careful*, which is minimizing your own values in favor of somebody else's. Being *careless* is exaggerating yourself and projecting your values onto somebody else's values. But caring is learning how to communicate your highest values in terms of their highest values. I showed her how to do that. I spent another hour and a half with her, till two o'clock in the morning helping her practice her communication skills in a caring manner.

The woman went home that night. Her husband was standing outside the door and said, "Where in the hell have you been?"

"I've been working with Dr. Demartini."

"Who in the hell is Dr. Demartini?"

"I've been working with Dr. Demartini to help me appreciate all that you've done for me in my life that I've never seen or acknowledged before."

"Oh. Well, God almighty, look how late it is. Let's go to sleep." He didn't beat her that night.

The next morning, she shared with him what she had learned at the program. She realized what she had done and what she'd been projecting onto him. She opened up and communicated more effectively according to and within his higher value system. She asked him to teach her how to build some financial stability and wealth, because she had been disempowering that area of her life.

Remember, in any area of your life where you don't empower yourself, somebody else overpowers you. If you don't develop your finances, somebody else will control you financially. If you don't develop your relationship, somebody else will control it. Somebody else is going to control any area where you don't take accountability and empower yourself.

Now the husband did not beat this woman; he took her to the seminar the next day. When she came back that next morning, she was crying, with a bunch of people around her. She said, "He didn't beat me last night. I've got a handle on what's going on." That day, she practiced some more on how to communicate in terms of his higher value system. She did some more internal work on herself involving some places in her childhood where she felt she had made a so-called mistake and was beating herself up over it. She found they weren't actually mistakes; she just didn't see the order in them. Over three years later, she had never been beaten once by her husband anymore.

The Illusion of Victimhood

It's not so much about what goes on in the outer world; it's what goes on in the inner world. Although that may be shocking to some people in a world that lives in a victim mentality, it is a more reflective understanding of the truth.

An ignorant person is inclined to blame others for his own misfortune. To blame oneself is proof of progress. But the wise individual never has to blame another or himself.
—Epictetus

I made that comment on television in New York City once. I was supposed to be on for eight minutes, but they gave me a whole hour on the show, because people were calling in, saying, "What about this victim and that victim?" I gave them solutions. Even the chief of police in New York, who was in the audience, was interested in what I was sharing, because he'd never thought of that paradigm. He had been assuming that the perpetrator or predator is the bad guy and the so-called innocent victim the good guy. But this is only the so-called mass conscious reality: the second we own our dynamic and become more accountable for our perceptions, decisions, and actions, we are free. Until we do, we're disassociating and disempowering people by imposing our illusive projections onto them. False attribution biases do not empower. It takes two to tango.

When you acknowledge the other individual for their role in your awakening, that individual shifts. We exercise a nonlocal influence on people as soon as we love them.

When we love people for who they are, they turn into who we love. When you try to project your value system onto them and expect them to be other than they are, this sets you up for what is unwisely, but commonly, called betrayal. Betrayal is projecting your values and expectations onto somebody else and expecting them to live by your value systems. They're guaranteed to betray you, because it's a projection of your values, not theirs. Others are not designed to live in your values. They are committed to the fulfillment of their own.

When you realize that other people have a set of values and you can only expect them to live by their highest values, you no longer set yourself up for betrayal.

In some respects, my late wife was the complementary opposite of me. She enjoyed sailing around the world, dining, writing her articles, socializing, shopping and getting manicures and pedicures, while I loved researching, writing, books, teaching, and flying. The more I loved working, the more she seemed to love relaxing and going to the spa. I could only guarantee that my wife would live according to her highest values. If I loved her for her highest values, not my own projected ones, I was free and felt love back. The second I did, she could be whoever she wanted to be, and my projection was no longer there. I did have the accountability to sell my higher values to her in terms of her own higher values when I wanted her to do something, but that was my responsibility; it wasn't hers. Otherwise, I would have been assuming that she was supposed to read my mind and live according to my values, which is unrealistic and becomes futile.

If I wanted my wife to come to a talk on atomic physics at a university and she had an option to get a manicure or a facial, she'll say, "I'll try, honey." What is she really saying? "I'm not going to be there. Heck no."

On the other hand, I could go up to her and say, "Honey, I'm presenting a speech in Madrid, Spain. They have one of the best spas there, and masseuses and pedicures and manicures. Then maybe afterwards, we can fly in a private jet over to Venice and walk through San Marco Square and listen to violins and have a romantic getaway." If I wanted her to do something, it was my accountability to sell her on the idea by talking in terms of her highest values; that was respectfully caring. If I honored her enough to care about her values and communicate mine in terms of hers instead of rejecting mine for hers, or hers for mine, I empowered and nurtured the relationship.

That's maturity. Some people will call it manipulation, but welcome to life. It is only called manipulation when your partner does not feel you have considered their higher values sufficiently and they are not winning in the exchange.

You may be doing this without realizing it. Children manipulate their parents in this way; parents also manipulate their children: "I'll do this if you do that." Somehow people got the idea that manipulation is bad; I'd rather just call it caring once it is done where both parties win. Manipulation has a devalued image when only one of the parties unfairly wins.

My wife would sometimes call and say, "Honey, I've set us up for a lovely dinner evening. We're going to Le

Cirque, where there's a big social evening engagement. It's $1,000 a head. I'd like you to take me and two other people. I think there may be some great speaking or consulting opportunities there." I'll gratefully shell out $4,000 for potential speaking and consulting possibilities. But if she says, "I just want to go to the dinner at Le Cirque," I don't know if I would have wanted to spend the money, because it's not enough value for me. If it hits and potentially fulfills my higher value system, I'll do it. We can call it whatever you want, but this is human behavior. Human behavior functions according to values. If you support someone else's values, they open up to you. If you challenge those values, they close down to you. When you love someone, you will experience a lovely balance of both.

I worked with a lady in New York City who was a very famous socialite. Her husband died. They had a 27,000-employee company whose main headquarters was in China. She had to take on that company now. She inherited about $60 million, and she has four homes around the world, all with staff. She had an apartment in New York. Her late husband had an ex-wife with a son who was out to get the inheritance money; this ex-wife sent the son over to the socialite's apartment to kill her that night. Now that's a pretty stressful day. On top of that, she was of European descent, so she was supposed to mourn for her husband for two years. Those were the unstated social rules she was supposed to live by. So we sat down and did eight hours' worth of work using the

Demartini Method to dissolve her grief and many other lingering emotional illusions.

The next day, the lawyer from the son who was out to dissolve the will contacted this woman, saying that he decided not to go forward with it. As for the company with 27,000 employees, somebody over the next few weeks rose to the occasion and was able to take over the leadership.

In short, the dynamics around us change when the dynamics within us change. When we come to equilibrium, equanimity and equity, the world around us changes.

We are surrounded by a magnificent world, but most people don't recognize or acknowledge that. They don't even know what surrounds them, because they keep projecting their subjectively biased illusions onto the external world. Their lives are filled with false attribution biases and moral hypocrisies.

I once worked with a couple where the man was dealing with a strong infatuation. The man was in La La Land. He told the woman, "I want to sacrifice my whole life for you. You're the most beautiful woman I've ever met. I'm going to divorce my wife, although I haven't even told her yet, and I'm going to let go of my children. I want to spend the rest of my life with you"—and he had just met her. Is that an infatuation? Is that seeing more positives than negatives? Absolutely. I spend hours cracking his fantasy and bringing him back down to a more balanced perception, so he gradually calmed down and grounded himself before doing more foolish, impulsive reactions. I asked him for the downsides of the new woman and the upsides of his wife, and leveled the playing field. His infatuation was broken, and he restabilized and appreciated his marriage. He had been blindsided by an illusion of one-sidedness. He was initially in a low emotional intelligence state, where he was ungoverned from within and therefore controlled from without.

3

Balancing Perceptions

To balance the polarities in emotions, I have developed a process called the Demartini Method. It involves balancing your perceptions of yourself and others until you reach complete equilibrium. In essence, everything that you see in the other, you discover that you actually own 100 percent in yourself. I've taken hundreds of thousands of cases through this process, and each time, each individual has the trait, action, or inaction they perceive and judge in the other when they are held accountable to be objective and get past their initial subjective biases. The seer, the seeing, and the seen are the same, because it was their projection in the first place. Again, what you point your finger at in others lies within.

The Demartini Method

Although we work very precisely and specifically with each individual and the trait, action, or inaction they judge in the Demartini Method, I will give the broad outlines of the process here.

When you read that every individual has the same trait they see in another, you may think, "No way." I took a lady through this process who was the head of a prison justice department in Canada; she challenged me on the spot. I brought her to the front of the room, with 200 people present.

This woman chose the individual that she was going to work on, who was an imprisoned serial killer. Believe it or not, she had to find out where *she* was a serial killer.

"No, there's no way," she said. "I've never killed anybody."

I said, "Look again."

"I've never killed anybody."

"Look again."

All of a sudden, it hit her. She realized who perceived her as a serial killer. She was a tough lady in the justice department. Some criminals knew that they would probably never get out of prison for the rest of their lives because of her strictness. A few of them committed suicide, and other inmates who knew them blamed her for their inmate's deaths. They perceived her as the soulless serial killer, because anybody who went in her prison was going to die. She became humble, realizing, "Oh my God, it's there; it's just another form."

Nearly four decades ago, I went through the *Oxford English Dictionary* and identified and underlined 4,628 individual human behavioral traits. I then thought of various individuals I knew that displayed or demonstrated each of those traits to the highest degree. I then reflected on my life and identified where and when I displayed or demonstrated every one of those traits within my own life. I found every one of them. I was kind and cruel, peaceful and wrathful, generous and stingy, and honest and dishonest. I had to face that I was all of them at different moments.

Everybody has every trait. The essence is the same, the traits are the same, but we are unique in our expression of them—according to our own unique set of values. Wisdom is knowing that everybody is like a holographic expression of the same essence, only in a unique form. I have helped my students and clients own more than a million traits, and it is eye-opening to discover this reflected truth about each of them.

The key is to identify where you display or demonstrate the same specific trait as does this other individual, as well as who perceives it in you. Go to the moments where and when you perceive yourself displaying or demonstrating this trait, past or present, and become aware of these previously unconscious instances, and who perceives you doing it, so you can realize that you are transparent: other people see it, but they still interact and even love you.

The next part is asking, what are the upsides, benefits, or advantages of that event, that occurrence, that trait? Say you are trying to find the benefit when someone else is inconsiderate in their verbal and physical response to you. You might discover upon looking deeper: "Well, it helped me to become more self-reliant. It helped me learn how to communicate more respectfully in terms of their value systems. It helped keep me from relying on somebody unless I'm willing to sell them on the value of what I want. It helped me learn to look for where another individual is helping me remain balanced and who's being overly considerate to me. When I start looking for the benefits of that lack of consideration, I realize that I'm being inconsiderate myself, because I'm expecting them to live by my value systems. I'm judging them according to my value systems, which itself is inconsiderate."

You simply stay accountable long enough to write down enough benefits until you can say, "I am now thankful to this individual for their behavioral trait. I have no desire to change them, and I hope my own child has that trait." If you can't do that, you haven't found enough benefits to neutralize the charge.

The value of going through this process is that the charge is gone. As long as the charge is there, it's running your life. Unless it's dissolved, it'll be there, possibly for decades: "Someone did something to me twenty-five years ago, and it's festering inside."

That's what some diseases are. That's what some cancer is: stored emotions sitting inside at the most primitive level. Cancer is sometimes the last-ditch effort of the human body to reveal to the soul and the mind what they haven't loved, often in early times of life.

Drawbacks and Benefits

Next, you probe and discover the drawbacks to you of this particular trait. Sometimes you imagine that another individual is generously giving and nicely mannered, but in fact they're generous only if your plea or behavior supports their values; otherwise, they can also be equally as stingy. Have you been stingy in certain areas of your life and generous in others? Have you been considerate at times and inconsiderate at others? The truth is, we're both. Every human being has a complete complement of traits and antitraits. Whenever you expect one without the other, you're living in a fantasy, and the social world around you will break it. A broken heart is a broken fantasy; it's designed to be that way—to break the myth that any situation is one-sided and to awaken us to the unity and simultaneity of opposites. An elevated emotional intelligence perceives both sides simultaneously.

Once we've acknowledged that we have this trait equally, we next find out whom it benefits. This dissolves fear and guilt, because you're also ascribing pleasures, benefits, and positives to what you've previously characterized as only painful, drawbacks, and negatives.

The next process in dissolving guilt is to see instances where you have displayed this same specific trait toward someone else and find out the many hidden benefits it provides to them. If you perceive you have displayed or demonstrated a so-called negative trait to someone, another individual, one or many, male or female, close or distant, real or virtual, simultaneously acted in the opposite way toward them. This awareness including both sides simultaneously frees you from the belief that you have hurt that individual in some way. You realize if you reject them, somebody else has supported them; if you support them, somebody has challenged them. Each perception involves a contrast of complementary opposites.

Then you turn the situation around. If you have played out a positive role for others, you ask, what are the simultaneous drawbacks to them? Say you try to be generous by giving them money. What's the drawback to other people? They become dependent on you; they have expectations; they lose touch with their own drive and creativity. Everything has a complement.

You don't get rid of the negative; you merely stuff it inside. If you put on an external facade of happiness, guess where the negative goes? It goes inside yourself. Your brain has an inner wisdom, which brings homeostasis and authenticity to the mind when it has unwisely assumed there is only a one-sided event.

The moral licensing effect is one such example, where the moment you do some act you feel proud of—say, working out hard—you simultaneously give yourself permission to overeat or overdrink to compensate, which simultaneously makes you feel ashamed enough to make you go and work out once again.

Antitraits

So far, you've perceived a given trait, action, or inaction in another individual and then reflected and discovered it equally within yourself. Then you have probed and discovered both the benefits and the drawbacks of this trait. The next step is finding in them the other half of the perception—the antitrait. You are to now find out where that same individual displays or demonstrates the opposite trait. If you've seen them as inconsiderate to you, where are they considerate to you? If you see them as intelligent, where have they been unintelligent? You keep digging and probing until it's 50/50: find where they have both the trait and the antitrait in equal quantities. If you still think they're more one way than the other, you remain polarized, or, if you're extremely imbalanced, with all-or-none thinking. Once they are balanced, the biased label goes, and a more objective perception of them emerges.

We all have areas of strength and weakness. I've studied principles concerning human behavior for decades, so I have accumulated some intelligence there, but when it comes to computer software, I'm a ditz; I don't know much at all. In short, everybody's an idiot in some respects and a genius in others; their hierarchy of values dictates where they have order and intelligence and where they have stupidity and chaos.

An example from my life: some people labeled my parents as inconsiderate because they dropped me off on the freeway when I was fourteen years old to hitchhike to California and eventually fly to Hawaii to ride big waves, because I couldn't make it in school. Some people thought that was absolutely terrible. Others thought it was great: the boy goes out and finds out how he can do it on his own; he learns how to be street-smart. You can label it either way, but all that happened is that I was dropped off along the freeway. The benefit was that I am where I am today. Someone else might see that as a drawback: some people may think I'm a contribution to the world; others may think

I'm not. In any event, they're all projecting aspects of themselves that they haven't owned and loved.

An ancient proverb (which I'm making up) says, I'd rather have the whole world against me than my own authentic self or soul. My soul is what counts. As long as I'm loving from the soul, that's what matters.

The next step in this process is what I call the great discovery: at the same time that someone is demonstrating a given trait or behavior to you, someone else is demonstrating the opposite. This is based upon the law of contrasts. If somebody is inconsiderate to you, who is at the exact same moment considerate to you? They could be one or many, male or female, close or distant, real or virtual.

First, you go to the moment where and when you perceive this individual demonstrating this specific trait. Then you identify exactly where and when you are at that moment of perception. Then get clear on exactly what they are doing: the content and context of the trait. Then you become very present and dig deeply into your unconscious mind to discover who is demonstrating the complementary opposite trait to you simultaneously. It will pop into your conscious mind intuitively if you are present in the moment of the perception. It is at the moment of perception that the conscious and unconscious minds split when you judge, and it is at this same synchronous moment they can become reintegrated when you love. Once you do, you realize that the only process that's occurring on the planet is equilibration. All people are being equilibrated so as to help them be authentic and to feel love.

This insight is a myth breaker. A woman may be angry with her husband because she thinks he should have behaved in one way or another. She's living by a myth, believing that if her husband acted that way, their life would be happier. In reality, it wouldn't. It would just be different: a new set of pains and pleasures.

If you are frustrated when someone doesn't behave in the way you would like, it is wise to ask yourself: "If this individual had done the exact opposite behavior to what he or she did, and he did exactly what I wanted him to do, what would be the drawback to me?" We come up with the drawbacks and neutralize the myth of how we believe they should have acted. As long as you're comparing another individual to some mythical reality, there's no way they can live up to it, because everybody's has a balance of each of the traits and antitraits. So we go into the moment of perception and we break the myth. We find out both the drawbacks and the benefits of someone else's behavior in order to neutralize the trait.

Using this method, you can dissolve emotional charges, so you don't have to carry them around all the time. You will get results in exact proportion to how thoroughly you do this method. If you don't own a trait—positive or negative—that you see in someone else, you're still storing a charge there. It is essential that it is owned and balanced 100 percent if you want it to be liberated. When I'm working with somebody one-on-one, or in my seminar program, we'll sit there as many minutes or hours as it takes, and nobody leaves until the emotional charges are completely dissolved 100 percent, quantitatively and qualitatively.

Tears of Inspiration

There are certain criteria for telling when the process is complete. If you have to ask whether it's done, it's not. One sign that it is complete is that the individual gets tears of inspiration. They cannot stop; the tears come pouring out of their eyes, because they have a realization, they become aware of a hidden order, their heart opens, and there's love. The room momentarily disappears, and the other individual they are doing the method on appears, because the practitioner tunes out of this outer sensory perception and into a transcendental or inner spiritual sense of the heart. It doesn't matter if the other individual is alive or has been dead for twenty years. They're now inwardly perceived to be present in front of you, and you're communicating your love and appreciation. As soon as you do, you have inspiration, you have openheartedness, there are tears. You feel lighter, weightless, integrated. You feel less brain noise, and you're present with that individual, no matter where they are, or if they're even still alive. You will be certain and grateful when this occurs.

The Origin of Emotions

Let me go further into why we have emotions in the first place. As far as we can trace, every living creature, all the way down to single-cell organisms, have the capacity to seek that which supports its sustenance and avoid that which threatens it. The single-cell organism uses processes called endocytosis, which takes in food and nutrients, and exocytosis, which removes waste and toxic materials. So it seeks that which is pleasurable and fulfilling and avoids that which is challenging and emptying. It seeks prey, which is food, and avoids predators, for which *it* is food. All living organisms have these characteristics, all the way up to human beings.

We're not unique in having emotions. In fact, all the emotions that human beings have, believe it or not, have also been found in the animals. Our animal nature is emotional. In essence, we have at least a triune brain. One element is a very ancient structure in the brain that deals with impulses and instincts, which govern our responses to prey and predators. The second element is the emotional center, the limbic brain. Finally, there is a neocortex, for reason and objectivity. We have layers of emotions, impulses, and instincts, which are survival mechanisms. We perceive ourselves in a survival mode when we have to have food or prey or are afraid of being eaten by a predator, which in today's world represents any form of highly supportive or challenging perception.

Knee-jerk reflex reaction is a term that refers to the sudden kicking movement of the lower leg in response to a sharp tap on the patellar tendon, which lies just below the kneecap. This type of response, known as a *stimulus response*, is unlearned, rapid, involuntary, predictable, and primitive. It has very few options: it either fires or it doesn't. It is all or none, black or white.

Another example is placing your hand on a hot stove. It would be unlikely that you'd need to think to remove your hand. Instead, it would tend to happen instinctively as a reaction to external stimuli.

Each of these reflex responses, over which you have little if any control, originate in the most primitive part of the brain. These instinctive (avoiding) and impulsive (seeking) responses are highly effective when fight or flight can mean the difference between life and death. However, most of your life likely doesn't warrant living in a constant state of fight or flight. This is especially important to understand if you would love to awaken your mastery and govern your life. Your emotional intelligence is what moderates or governs such survival-based reflexive behaviors.

Here's why.

When you are functioning from those lower parts of the brain, you're likely to have limited potential, with few options and little freedom. You'll also tend to have very little control over your perceptions and actions, because you mostly react. You tend not to think about mitigating risk or making objective and balanced or more prudent decisions.

On the other hand, as you go forward, up into the very front of the brain (the prefrontal cortex in your forebrain, aka the *executive center*), there are massive amounts of interneurons which interact by means of associations. If you are thinking with this part of the brain, you'll be more likely to reflect on how you want to act instead of reflexively reacting. This is where you activate your leadership, genius, creativity, objectivity, strategic planning, and mind mastery. It could be considered the governing center of your emotional intelligence.

In short, at the lower, the most primitive level of the brain and spinal cord, you have more basic and simple *reflexes*. At the higher, most advantaged part of the brain, you have *reflection*.

Reflection indicates that you stop, process, think about an action, decide, strategically plan what you're going to do, mitigate risks, and control, govern, or moderate your responses. When you're in the more advanced part of the brain, you have *self-governance*, because you are able to take command of what you perceive or sense and decide what to do with it.

When you're using the lower, more primitive part of the brain, you're likely to be in survival and become a victim of your environment and your history. But when you let your executive center take command, you become a master of your destiny.

If we're infatuated with something, we fear its loss. If we're resentful toward something, we fear its gain. All of our emotions are derived from these two primary ones: seek and avoid. Emotions are imbalanced, polarized perspectives that show up as responses of seeking or avoidance. All emotions are basically variations of those responses. They are symptoms of an incomplete awareness due to survival-based subjective biases.

Emotional Intelligence

These insights help us see further into the nature of emotional intelligence. Emotional intelligence is the ability to have self-governance over your emotional reactions and have high self-awareness and self-reflection about your perceptions. It enables you to monitor, govern, and synchronously balance your perceptions and actions.

If you are in a highly polarized state, in which you're perceiving many more positives than negatives or more negatives than positives, the seeking or the avoidance mechanism is active, and you're out of control; you're ungoverned. In this moment you have low emotional intelligence. Emotional intelligence is the ability to govern and moderate your instincts and impulses. Your emotional intelligence is proportional to your ability to self-govern.

We differ from other species in having the capacity to use intuition and reason in the brain's executive center: we can employ foresight, plan, and mitigate potential future risks or perceptions of imbalance. If we have an imbalanced perspective in the moment, the lower brain systems come online and cause us to react, and we won't easily be able to override them.

The alternative is to anticipate the stimuli that could cause those reactions in advance and balance out our perceptions, because imbalanced perceptions cause these emotions. Emotions are imbalanced perceptions or perspectives.

The brain is set up in layers. Scientists used to describe the brain as a *recapitulated structure*. If you take a glass and stick another glass on top, and another glass on top of that, you have a recapitulated structure; you're putting layers upon layers. The same is true of the brain. Nature doesn't throw away the old layers: we still need them to respond to distress. We just have new layers on top of the older ones. Actually, all vertebrates have each of the layers, but they simply progressively developed and became expanded through the evolutionary phyla. We as human beings have more expanded telencephalic forebrains for intuition and reason as well as self-governance.

Because of the way the brain is set up, the lower emotional impulse and instinct center has larger-diameter neurons, which conduct neural impulses more rapidly. They will react as a survival mechanism before you have time to reason through the situation. I know of only a few ways of overruling that effect. One such way is exercising foresight, going through your life for previous emotional reactions, identifying those moments, looking for any history of chain reactions, going back to the earliest ones, and balancing them out. If your responses are neutral, when somebody comes along that previously would have irritated you, your brain won't have a subconscious storage of an imbalance, causing you to react in the more primitive part of the brain. You automatically come from an action orientation instead of reaction.

Phobias and Philias

If you have a *phobia* or fear, you are assuming that in your imagined future, you will experience more pains than pleasures, more losses than gains, more negatives than positives. The ratios of negatives to positives are imbalanced in favor of the former.

Conversely, if you have a *philia* (from an ancient Greek word for *attractive puppy love*), that is, an infatuation with something, you are assuming that in the future, you will experience more positives than negatives, more gains than losses, more pleasures than pains. Again there is imbalance.

Whenever you have an imbalanced perspective, the primitive part of the subcortical brain comes on line and reacts. By contrast, foresight enables you to balance out your perceptions of anticipated events and see the benefits to the ones you consider negative and the drawbacks of those you consider positive, so you can transcend and over-rule such polarized responses. The executive center, the reasoning part of the brain, overrules the emotions, and you become a master of destiny instead of a victim of history.

The key to the mastery of life and high emotional intelligence is through foresight, not hindsight. Humans have the capacity to overrule spontaneous emotions if they are trained to do so. Strategic planning and anticipating future events are what make leaders, leaders. They're thinking ahead. They overrule paradoxes.

There's no reason to beat yourself up about emotional responses. They're feedback mechanisms to let you know that you have an imbalanced perspective. Every event has two sides. We've all had experiences that we thought were terrible; a day, a week, a month, a year later, we realize that they were also magnificent. Conversely, we've all had events that we thought were terrific and then looked back and found that there were also downsides to them. If you train your mind to see both sides simultaneously, you will reduce the probability of storing a history of imbalances in your subconscious mind that make you vulnerable to external manipulation and over-emotional reactions.

Often we have people and events running us from the outside because we've never balanced our mind on the inside. We've taken an event and automatically assumed it's traumatic, terrible, or evil without stopping to look at the blessings and benefits. Until you do, your memory of this event is going to keep running you. You're going to be trapped, because you haven't taken the time to balance and govern your perceptions, experiences, and decisions.

In my seminar program the Breakthrough Experience, I show people how to take a traumatic—or terrific—event and see the other side. If you're seeing one without the other, you have an imbalanced perspective. You're not seeing what's actually there; you're seeing your own subjectively stored baggage and delusions projected onto what's there.

It's a matter of knowing how to ask the right questions to balance out your perceptions. It's also a matter of realizing that if you're triggered by an event, it means you've got something in the past that has still not been balanced. The present event is associated with the past one and is generating a reaction to protect you from something that you thought was painful or, on the other hand, that hooked you with perceived positives.

If you are hooked by positives, you will keep going into relationships that are characterized by infatuation, even though you know they aren't working. If you're being hooked by unsatisfactory relationships over and over, it's because your subconscious mind has stored previous experiences of a pleasure without a pain. Again, whenever you perceive a pain without a pleasure or a pleasure without a pain, that perception is sitting in your subconscious mind, ready to resurface again and keep you repeating this behavior. The more extreme these initially perceived events were, the lower the emotional intelligence you will display when they are once again triggered.

This pattern is reverberating and resurfacing to let you know that those earlier pieces of information have never been balanced. You now have the opportunity to go in with your executive center, ask quality questions, and balance those experiences. The more you balance, the less likely you are to have these reactions or build or beat yourself up about them. These reactions are feedback mechanisms to guide you to learn the art of balancing out your perceptions. The mastery of this questioning and answering process partly determines your level of emotional intelligence.

4

Values and the Void

~~~~~~

U p to this point, I've spoken occasionally about values—particularly the urgent need to live by your own values and not someone else's. Again, frequently telling yourself "I should," "I ought to," and so on is a sign that you're living by values that you have absorbed from without rather than coming from within.

Every human being lives with a set of values that is unique to himself or herself. You can easily tell what is highest on this list: it is what you are spontaneously inspired to do or fulfill. You don't have to tell yourself, "I should," because you innately love doing it.

My highest values are teaching, researching, writing, and traveling. I love these activities, so no one has to tell me to do them. I have little interest in driving or cooking, so I turn these jobs over to others. This isn't being unfair to these individuals: they take on these tasks because they are aligned with their own highest values.

If greater numbers of individuals in the world were to work and act congruently with their own highest values, the level of human fulfillment would be greater than it is now.

But what about a task you perceive to be undesirable? Actually, that same task isn't undesirable to everyone. You might find it unfulfilling, for example, to work as a garbage collector in Mexico City. But writer Joseph Sorrentino was observing some Mexican garbagemen and got a very different picture. In *Mexico News Daily,* he observes, "I often see them eating lunch while standing next to a truck overflowing with trash. How they're able to stand the smell is beyond my comprehension. Clearly, a very tough job undertaken by some very tough people."

One day he sees three garbagemen sitting in the back of a truck,

> The very back where the garbage is stuffed. The truck is full. Of garbage. And they're sitting right at the edge of the pile, probably on top of some of it.
>
> I don't know if this was a family, but it could've been.
>
> They were two men and a boy: an older man in his late 50s, another man looking to be in his late 30s and a kid around 10. So, yeah, I figure it could've been three generations. I like to think that it was.
>
> What really caught my attention was the kid, who was talking animatedly. He must have been telling funny stories because the other two men were laughing. Hard. This is while they're all sitting at the edge of

a pile of trash in the back of a garbage truck which, I'm certain, smelled awful.

Talking and laughing like they hadn't a care in the world. Just having a grand old time. And it was impossible to see them and not question just what in the hell the rest of us are doing, especially us Americans who are constantly pursuing happiness.

I had the feeling that those three guys, sitting there in the back of that garbage truck, they weren't pursuing happiness. Somehow, and I really wish I knew how, they'd caught that.

These garbagemen probably don't share my own interests or values: they would no doubt regard teaching, researching, and writing as unmitigated torture.

It's the same in your life. There are tasks and jobs that you simply dislike and prefer not to do: you avoid doing them if at all possible. You also have actions that you are spontaneously inspired to do. You won't procrastinate; instead, you'll make and take time for them. These are likely your highest values.

Other People's Values

Some individuals find it difficult to identify their highest values because they think they "should" be different from what or who they truly are. Their subordination to other outer authorities is clouding the clarity of what and who they truly are.

You may be trying to live in someone else's values. For example, you may perceive that you "should" have family as your highest value instead of work. Or perhaps you think you "should" have spirituality as your highest value instead of physical well-being or wealth building.

This situation may have come about because some people in your life have been telling you what your highest values and priorities "should" be. You may be allowing their voices to enter your head and cloud the clarity of your own true value hierarchy. If this is the case, you may not be honoring your own true highest values. You may be trying to live and act in ways or in areas where you are least spontaneous, productive, and inspired.

Another possibility: as we've seen, we often minimize ourselves in respect to other people and put them on pedestals, and as a result we sometimes inject their values into our life. We compare ourselves to them and think we're not as high in achieving as they are. Instead of living according to our highest values, we attempt to live according to theirs. Here too, we are disempowering ourselves: we're trying to do what does not intrinsically inspire us.

You may also be trying to get others to live according to *your* highest values. Whenever you expect others to live by your set of values or expect yourself to live by someone else's, you're likely to experience futility. No one can sustainably live according to someone else's values, because it goes against what's intrinsic to them.

When some activity is congruent with what is highest on your unique set of values, you are spontaneously inspired to carry it out. You don't need to be reminded, incentivized, or motivated externally; you're inspired internally, which is why some individuals refer to their highest value as their calling in life, or their métier, or *telos*. (I will say more about the telos later.)

Congruence and Values

The difference between living an inspired life and a life that requires external motivation has to do with the degree of congruency between our goals and intentions on the one hand and our highest values on the other.

If your goals are congruent with your highest values, you are inspired, and you achieve. When you achieve, you gain confidence in yourself, and you discover or perceive that the world is perceptually working on your behalf. You're no longer a victim of your history. You become a master of your destiny. And you are grateful.

This is the inspired life. When people live congruently with their own highest values, they wake up their inner geniuses, and their innovation and creativity begin to blossom.

Certainty in your life is directly proportionate to the congruency between your goals or objectives and your highest values. Whenever we subordinate ourselves to outer influential authorities and inject their values into our lives, we dissipate our potentiality. We scatter and doubt ourselves. We start to think, "I don't know, I'm not, and I can't." As a result, we live with moral dilemmas and internal conflicts. We tell ourselves, "I *should* be doing this; I *ought* to be doing this; I'm *supposed* to be doing this" instead of "I love doing this, and I'm inspired to do this."

When you love doing something, there's no inertia. The inertia in your life is directly proportionate to the lack of congruence between your intentions and actions and your highest value. If they are incongruent, entropy breaks you down.

I believe that many symptoms in your body are trying to offer you feedback. Whenever we're not living by our highest value but are going into lower, injected, or derivative values, we automatically create physiological symptoms. Most symptoms—of any kind—are feedback mechanisms telling you to refine and be yourself and live congruently with your highest values.

Authenticity emerges when there is congruency between your goals and intentions and your highest values. You become the masterful author of your life to the degree of your congruency and authenticity. The most meaningful and purposeful way we can live is congruently with our own genuine highest values. When we're doing that, nobody has to motivate us; we're inspired from within. We awaken our leadership, we become accountable, we give ourselves permission to shine, and we have more inner freedom and less constraint from authority.

When we're not living according to our highest values, we require outside coercion to motivate us. We become frustrated, and this frustration is a sign from the world around us to lead us back toward what's truly authentic to ourselves: a state in which both our service and our rewards are maximal.

In short, if you frequently tell yourself, "I *should* be doing this" or "I *should* be this kind of individual," your congruency may be low. The same is true if you find yourself routinely resistant or indifferent to your work. If you're doing what you truly love, you're much more likely to be enthusiastic and inspired to serve and be fairly rewarded.

Your Highest Value

Every human being, regardless of age, gender, or culture, is living with a set of priorities, a set of values: items or objectives that are most and least important in their life. That hierarchical set of intrinsic to extrinsic values is unique to each individual. (If any two people are identical, one of them is not necessary on the planet.) Each of us is like a snowflake, a retinal pattern, or a voice print—entirely unique.

No two people can have exactly the same set of values, although they may be similar. You may say, "Business is important" or "Family is important," and someone else may make the same statement, but these can have entirely different meanings to each of you. Every individual's set of values is like a set of fingerprints.

This hierarchy of your values ranges from what is most important to least important, from what is higher in value to what is lower. This set of values dictates your perceptions of the world, because you are filtering your reality through this hierarchy.

What Is an Intrinsic Value?

As you go down the list of values from higher to lower, they become more and more extrinsic—that is, determined or derived from the outside.

Your sensory input goes through your sensory receptors into the spinal cord, or brain stem, and ascends to the higher areas of your brain. This input then passes through the thalamus, where it passes through a highest-value-based filtering process, which determines whether the impressions go up into the cortex (where you'll be consciously aware of them) or into the amygdala (where you'll have partly conscious and unconscious, impulsive or instinctive responses).

You tend to absorb, retain, and apply information that you associate with your highest values. In these instances, you tend to make decisions more efficiently, and you're more likely to act promptly. Hence in the areas of your highest values, you're *disciplined*, *reliable*, and *focused*. Conversely, you'll *procrastinate* and *hesitate* about what you progressively value less.

Your highest value is that which is most important in your life at any moment. It is the most intrinsic value: your identity revolves around it; it's how you identify yourself. You will be spontaneously inspired to act upon it.

Values are the foundation of my work and teaching. My own highest intrinsic value is teaching on the mastery of human behavior. I teach seven days a week, sometimes for eighteen hours a day. I'm spontaneously inspired to do it. No one has to extrinsically motivate me to do what I love most, to teach.

Finding out what's highest on your hierarchy of values, and living congruently according to it will allow you to genuinely become inspired to take persistent action and excel most.

Although you may not be conscious of it, your life demonstrates what your intrinsic value is. Finding it out, acknowledging it, and prioritizing your life toward it consciously is very empowering, because whenever you act in accordance with your highest value, your self-worth increases, your achievements go up, and you expand your space and time horizons. Moreover, your capacity for leadership emerges. I'm a leader in the field of human behavior and maximizing human awareness and potential because it's my intrinsic value.

Living by your highest value has neurological effects. When you're living by your highest value, your blood, glucose, and oxygen flow into your forebrain, and you wake up your executive center, which is the source of your inspired vision, your life's strategic plan, and your spontaneous action. Those who are inspired by a vision have more vitality than those who are not. Those with a vision flourish, and those without a vision perish.

When you're living by your highest values, you're more likely to be fair and objective in your relationships. You're not biasing yourself with superiority or inferiority complexes, and you're more likely to perceive yourself as equal to other people. You're also more likely to love and respect them for who they are and communicate caringly with dialogue.

When you're living by your highest value, you act spontaneously; you don't need to be motivated externally. If you need to be motivated to do what you say is important, then what you say is important isn't all that important to you.

Living according to your highest value maximizes your resilience and adaptability, because you're more neutrally stabilized. When you're highly polarized, you fear the loss of what you label "good" and the gain of what you label "bad." When you're living by your highest value, you transcend both labels "good" and "bad"; being objective, you can see both sides simultaneously.

Living by your highest value also enables you to transcend ethical labels. You don't judge people; you love them. You also realize that every human being (including yourself) encompasses all traits and both polarities. You have reflective more than deflective awareness.

You Can Live by Your Intrinsic Value

Your hierarchy of values is evolving and can change, incrementally or cataclysmically, and will continue to do so throughout your life.

When I was a child, first baseball was important, then surfing was important to me, and now, for the last fifty years, teaching, researching, writing, traveling, and what I've learned about human behavior and universal laws have been important to me. Even so, I might have another new value evolve in the future.

Your identity revolves around your highest, most intrinsic value. It's where you most grow your knowledge, and you become the expert in that area. What's highest on your hierarchy of values gives you a *core competence*, giving you a competitive and comparative advantage there.

Your highest value is also your teleological purpose. (*Teleological* comes from the Greek *telos* or *end in mind*.) Your intrinsic value, your real identity, is nonderivative: it doesn't come from outside shoulds and musts from society. It an intrinsic, spontaneous action, bringing your mind to into objective balance. In this way, you synchronize and maximize the circadian rhythms in your physiology. It balances your autonomics. You empower your wellness and every other area of your life.

Your ontological identity, your teleological purpose, and your epistemological knowledge revolve around this highest value. So do your areas of expertise, leadership skills, expanded awareness, and level of enlightenment. That's your identity. That's your true, authentic self.

Low- versus High-Priority Tasks

Any task that needs external motivation to get someone to act is a derivative, extrinsic value. In your hierarchy of values, your highest and most intrinsic values override your lower, extrinsic ones.

I learned a long time ago not to waste time on low-priority tasks. Fill your day with high-priority activities, and delegate lower-priority duties to other specialists. If a task is high in their values, they'll be inspired to do them, and you'll liberate yourself from what you consider drudgery.

What's higher on your values may be lower on someone else's values and vice versa. You will want to delegate lower-priority tasks to them because those tasks are inspiring to them, and they will delegate their lower-priority tasks to you because they are inspiring to you. This utilitarian matrix, which is called a *transactional relationship*, will help both of you work most effectively and efficiently in accomplishing your dreams. In this way, you'll surround yourself with inspiring people, each doing what they love.

External motivation is not a solution for human beings. It's a symptom. It's a sign of activities that are not perceived to be inspiring or meaningful—a life of quiet desperation, not a life of inspiration.

Theory X and Theory Y

Douglas McGregor, a professor of management at MIT in the 1950s and '60s, noticed the differences between workers that were self-driven and those that required external motivation in their work. He called them Theory Y and Theory X people respectively. With Theory Y people, their job descriptions and goals were perceived to be congruent with and assisting them in fulfilling their own highest values and intentions. As a result, they didn't have to be externally motivated. Theory X people were those who could not see how their job duties helped them fulfill their own highest values and mission, and they required costly external incentives.

Whenever we react, we do so because we believe that it will provide us with more advantages than disadvantages and more rewards than risks. Almost every decision we make is based on that premise. Even when we say we didn't act intentionally, we did, because we unconsciously believed that it supported our values, regardless of what we may say. Our actions reflect our values sometimes more than our words do. Whenever you make a mistake, it's unlikely to be due to your own values: it can only be due to the injection of somebody else's values. The degree that you subordinate yourself to outer influences and give power to other people is the degree to which you think you're making mistakes. This erodes your confidence and certainty. You will also think other people make mistakes when you compare their actions to your own set of projected values.

For everyone on the planet with a set of values, there's somebody with a completely opposite set. What one wants to build, the other wants to destroy, and the combination of the two create transformation, which makes the world work—antiabortion and proabortion, progun and antigun, provaccine and antivaccine, procapitalism and anticapitalism, and so on.

The same principles apply in social structures: our collective hierarchy of values dictates our social destiny. This hierarchy determines how we collectively see the world through our senses and act upon it with our motor functions. It also determines where we're going to excel and where we're going to end up being somewhat deficient in the global marketplace.

We have the capacity to excel. People doubt themselves because they have both a habit and a history of attempting to not live congruently with their highest values. As soon as they identify their true highest values and set objectives that match, they gain amazing vitality and regain their confidence. Why? Because your vitality is directly proportionate to the vividness of your vision. And your vision become crystal clear to the degree that it is free of outer injected values, which cloud its clarity. Any detail that's left out of your vision becomes a clouding obstacle and a challenge.

Someone who knows their true highest values and sets goals that are congruent with them awakens clear vision. You know you have a clear vision if you can articulate it to somebody concisely and fluently, and they can see the vision and want to be part of it because of the enthusiasm and inspiration you have for it. It's a matter of ordination, not subordination. Leaders are born out of congruency.

The Limits of Authority

You may have been raised with authority figures, starting with your mom and dad. Sigmund Freud (1856–1939), the founder of psychoanalysis, said that whenever we inject the values of an authority figure into our life and act in ways that we think align with these values, we'll swell up in pride. Whenever we act in ways that we think go against them, we'll beat ourselves in shame and judge ourselves. This injected authority becomes what Freud called a *super-ego*, which judges our so-called moral actions. There's no way out of that prison as long as we subordinate ourselves to external authorities. Few individuals make it through the preconventional, conventional, and postconventional stages of moral development to the final stage of transcendence where they live more by eternal universal laws than by only transient human rules and injunctions. Few self-actualize or trailblaze a new path for humanity.

Great philosophers knew that the only way out of this prison that Plato called the "cave" was to have reflective awareness: the realization that what they see in other people is also within them. Plato's student Aristotle also showed his pupils that whatever they saw in the world around them was a reflection of themselves. When they fully saw that quality in themselves, they no longer subordinated themselves to some external authority; they owned the traits they saw externally. Any trait that we see in others that we have been too humble or too proud to admit we have is a power and trait we've disowned. We think that we want to be like our mentors, but if we look deeper, we discover that we already have all the traits that they have. We're not honoring them, because they're in *our* form, not theirs. Whenever we try to live according to others' set of values, we'll think that there's something wrong with us. We are here to honor our own values and not subordinate to theirs. To live congruently according to our own highest values while simultaneously serving others in their highest values in a fair and sustainable manner is the key to high emotional intelligence and mastery.

The German philosopher Arthur Schopenhauer has been quoted as saying that we become our true selves to the degree that we make everyone and everything else ourselves. That means whatever we see in other people around us, we have within us. We're not here to minimize ourselves or sit in anyone's shadow. We're here to recognize that magnificence inside ourselves. To the degree that we do, we awaken our leadership.

Whenever we're carrying out some activity that is perceived as not helping us fulfill our highest values, our confidence erodes. That's why one of the greatest questions we could ever ask ourselves is, *how is whatever we're sensing, whatever we're doing, helping us fulfill our highest values?* If you do this, certainty and gratitude emerge.

Amazing questions awaken true authenticity and create amazing lives. Although we may not yet be full masters of our destiny, we're not here to be victims of our history. In any area of life that we don't empower, we will attract other people to overpower us until we get frustrated enough to empower that area.

That's why we're here to be grateful. Anything we can't be grateful for is still our burdening illusion. Plato said all learning is recollection. We already have the potentiality, even though we don't recognize it. I don't know what the limit is; I don't think human beings have reached it. Many times, people who come from the humblest setting carry out extraordinary accomplishments.

I recently had the opportunity to work with a lovely young lady who was having some challenges in school. She had a dream, but she found it difficult to see how her schooling was helping her fulfill that dream. She excelled at the class that she could see as connected to her dream, but she couldn't see how the rest of the classes were connected to it.

I spent the evening showing this young woman how every one of those classes could help her fulfill her dream. Her energy level went up, her eyes lit up, her enthusiasm came alive, and she saw new possibilities. From the following day on, her engagement at school went up, as well as her grades.

As soon as we can see how whatever we're doing is linked to and helping us fulfill our highest-value-based mission, our vitality and empowerment grow. We are now eager to live an extraordinary life. That's our true nature, and our destiny. Anything less is a lie. The higher our congruency, the greater our emotional intelligence, and the greater our achievements and fulfillment.

It is wise to either do what we love through delegating or love what we do through linking.

The Ultimate End

I call the highest priority in your life your *highest value*. It's what's most important in your life. The ancient Greeks called this the *telos*, which means *the ultimate end in mind*.

Every human being at any moment has a telos. The ancient Greeks understood that this subject was so important that they devoted an entire discipline to it, which is called *teleology*. It is the study of meaning and purpose. The telos is built into the equation of the human experience. This highest value is what we are inspired from within to live. It is, therefore, called an *intrinsic value*, meaning that nobody has to motivate us from the outside to do it. Nobody has to motivate you to do what is truly highest on your hierarchy of values. If you're ten years old and your highest value is video games, nobody has to get you up in the morning to play video games.

Neurologists call the end and outermost layer of the brain, the forebrain, which is the most advanced part, the *telencephalon*. We've already seen the meaning of *telos*: *end*. *Encephalos* is the ancient Greek word for *brain*, so this is the part of the brain designed to work toward the telos. Somebody who lives according to their telos employs this telencephalic part of the brain. It is maximally developed to the degree that we live according to our highest value; at that point, we have the greatest degree of authenticity, creativity and innovation.

As you go down the list of values to what is less important, you increasingly require outside motivation to act. This is called an *extrinsic value*: a task that you require outside motivation to do. In a recent article in *Psychology Today*, Geoff Smart writes, "Wondering 'how to motivate employees' is a management fail."

Productivity, as we've seen, is directly proportionate to an individual's congruence with their own highest value. Every decision you make is based on what you believe will give you the greatest advantage or disadvantage, the greatest reward over risk at any moment in time. You will only act if you believe it will provide you with more advantages than disadvantages, and that's based on your highest value or telos. Your telos, working through your prefrontal cortex and amygdala, is your decision maker. It's the pontifical component of your psyche. When you act according to your telos as you understand it, you're able to make decisions quickly, act upon them, and stay with them over the long term. In his book *Think and Grow Rich*, Napoleon Hill said that successful people make decisions quickly and stick to them. That's because they're aligned with their own highest value.

In contrast to teleology, which has to do with ultimate ends, *technology* deals with means to the end. Technology was the tool that human beings developed to effect the fulfillment of highest values. With their innovation and creativity, they generated tools and technologies to advance the fulfillment of their values more effectively and efficiently. Your emotional intelligence is heightened to the same degree that you live congruently with your highest value or telos.

An individual purpose is the most effective and efficient pathway to fill the greatest number of voids with the greatest amount of value, because whatever is most valuable to us stems from the voids in our life. As Aristotle said, whatever we think is missing is most important: it's our voids that yearn to be filled. Consequently, whatever is our greatest void is the source of what we perceive to be our greatest value. If we don't think we have enough money, we seek money. If we don't think we have enough relationships, we seek relationships. If we don't think we have market share, we seek market share. The void drives the value. We want to import it into our sphere of awareness and influence because we assume and feel they are empty. When we fill it, we're satisfied. Then, as psychologist Abraham Maslow showed with his hierarchy of needs, we go on to the next need, the next void.

Whatever we are too proud or too humble to admit that we display or demonstrate that we perceive in others what we admire or despise becomes the source of our voids. These are disowned parts. Ultimately, nothing is missing within us, but we perceive these traits, actions, or inactions to be missing. When we judge others and disown traits, we create empty voids that drive or determine our values, to ultimately be owned through reflection and eventually love of what we previously judged.

5

Discerning Your Values

Now that we've gone into discussing values in some detail, we can see how they relate to emotional intelligence. *Emotional intelligence means living congruently with your own highest and most intrinsic values.* Otherwise, you will be living under extrinsic values, whether you acquired them from your parents, society, or some ultimately irrelevant set of ideals, which will require outside motivation to get you to act upon them.

How, then, do we know whether we are living congruently with our highest values? The answer isn't that difficult to come by: as much as possible, we spend our time living according to those values. This is true even and especially if we are haunted by guilt telling us that we *should* be involved in a completely different arena. A man believes that his family is his highest priority. If he is spending eighty-four hours a week working in the office, this is unlikely to be the case. Another man thinks that his highest value has to do with wealth and power, but if he spends most of his time watching cartoons on TV, we have reason to doubt him. It is what your life truly demonstrates that matters most when determining your hierarchy of values. Your actions speak louder than your words.

The Demartini Value Determination Process

What if you're still not sure about your highest value?

To help you find it, I've developed the Demartini Value Determination Process.

When I was twenty-three years of age and earning my doctoral degree, I came to realize how significant the hierarchy of values was in human perceptions, decisions, actions, drive, and achievement.

I searched for and found various ways of determining what people called "values." But the methods I discovered seemed to be too subjective and socially idealistic—more geared to what individuals wanted to believe in than to the actual values by which they were living. So I began researching an alternative way to more objectively determine values, filtering out social pressure and idealisms.

The Demartini Value Determination Process evolved over the years to what it is today. It consists of thirteen questions that will more clearly reveal what your life demonstrates as most valuable to you: your highest priorities or your hierarchy of highest values.

You can go through this process step by step on my website (www.drdemartini.com), but I will give the details in a slightly abbreviated form here as well. Just follow the directions. You can write the answers out in this book, but you might prefer to do it on a separate piece of paper, or on my more comprehensive free and private online version, which you can date and save. Later you may want to take the test again; possibly you will find different results, since your hierarchy of values is gradually evolving.

1. YOUR INTIMATE OR PERSONAL SPACE

The study of *proxemics* divides your individual space into:

Your intimate space, which is up to one and a half feet around you.

Your personal space, which is up to four feet around you.

Your social space, which is up to twelve feet around you.

Your public space, which is beyond twelve feet around you.

What items, objects, or individuals do you fill your intimate, personal, or virtual space with most? What do these items really represent or mean? What are they actually being used for most? What is the primary purpose for them being there?

Items that are not highly important to you are tossed or placed distantly in the trash, the attic, or the garage. Look carefully at what you have in your home or office and see what you display in your most valued space. Objects that are highly important to you, you will keep in your possession, close by, or somewhere where you can frequently sense and interact with them. You may even be wearing some of them. So look at how you fill your personal and professional space.

If you walked into your home or company office space and looked carefully, what would you see? What does your intimate, personal or professional life demonstrate as most important?

- Do you see your computer or business materials?
- Do you see business awards, certificates, books, reference materials?
- Do you see sports trophies?
- Do you see design items, paintings, arts, crafts?
- Do you see animals and pictures and books on animals?
- Do you see books and magazines on building wealth?
- Do you see pictures of your children or even your actual children?

Look carefully right now and ask yourself how you fill your intimate, personal, or professional space. What three items stand out? Keep each of your answers concise: one, two, or three words. Think what each of these items specifically represent to you and what is their dominant use.

Now ask yourself these three questions:

How do you fill your intimate or personal space most?

_____

How do you fill your intimate or personal space second most?

_____

How do you fill your intimate or personal space third most?

_____

2. YOUR TIME

Look carefully and accurately at how you spend your time. What are the three areas of life where you spend most of your time? You will make time for what is really important to you, and you will run out of time for what isn't.

Even though you may say, "I don't have time for what I really want to do," the truth is that you are busy doing what is most important to you and just may not know it. What you think you want to be doing isn't necessarily what is truly most important and valuable to you. You will find or make time for what you truly consider most important.

Look carefully at how you spend your time. Look at how you structure your twenty-four-hour day. What do you most often do in your sixteen to eighteen hours of awake time? You will allocate your time for activities that are important to you: you will divide up your days according to your true priorities, conscious or unconscious. If a task is not important, you will keep putting it off until tomorrow.

- Do you work ten hours of the day?
- Do you socialize four hours a day?
- Do you read or study three hours a day?
- Do you spend three hours a day with your children?
- Do you spend several hours on shopping?
- Do you work out, do yoga, or train for two hours a day?

Make sure you are honest and objective about how you spend your waking hours most. What are the top three answers?

Answer these questions:

How do you spend your time the most?

_____

How do you spend your time the second most?

_____

How do you spend your time the third most?

_____

If you are honest with yourself and look objectively, you will already begin to see a pattern emerging.

3. YOUR ENERGY

Next, look at how you spend your energy and what energizes you most. You will have and experience elevated energy for what's truly highest on your values list. You will run out of energy for what isn't important to you.

Look at where you feel most vital and enthused in your day-to-day activities. Tasks that are low on your list of values will tend to drain you and put you to sleep, whereas tasks that are high on your list of values will tend to awaken and energize you.

- Is it being of service at work?
- Is it solving problems that make a difference in other people's lives?
- Is it working out and getting fit?
- Is it socializing?
- Is it cooking and entertaining for friends or loved ones?
- Is it shopping?

- Is it reading a great book or learning about what inspires you?
- Is it leading or managing people at work or at home?

When you are carrying out an activity throughout the day that is truly highest on your list of values—something that you love and are inspired by—you will have more energy at the end of the day than when you started.

Look carefully and honestly at what most energizes you, what you spend most of your energy on, and what you most consistently have energy for. Answer the following questions:

What energizes you the most? What do you most easily and consistently find or have energy for?

_____

What energizes you second most? What do you second most easily and consistently find or have energy for?

_____

What energizes you third most? What do you third most easily and consistently find or have energy for?

_____

4. YOUR MONEY

The next value determinant is how you spend your money. What do you spend most of your money and your financial resources on? Where is your income going, first most, second most and third most?

You will feel reluctant to spend money on items you perceive to be unimportant or of low value. If some items mean a lot to you, you will certainly figure out a way to pay for them. You create or find money for items that are truly valuable to you. You might even be considered to be cheap when you do not want to spend your money on objects that are too low on your priority list. You don't want to part with your money for them.

- Do you spend your money mostly on your home and security?
- Do you spend it on your business development?
- Do you spend it on clothes and accessories for your appearance?
- Do you spend it on specialized education?
- Do you spend it on social activities or events?
- Do you spend it on entertainment?

Look at how you spend your money, or how it is being spent most. Answer the three following questions:

How do you spend your money the most?

_____

How do you spend your money second most?

_____

How do you spend your money third most?

_____

As you fill in the answers to these first four value determinants, you may find that some of the answers are going to be the same or similar. This indicates that you are on track with this process: you are pretty congruent, and you are consistently working in areas that are more important to you. When answered honestly and objectively, these value determining questions begin to reveal a clear pattern of priority.

5. ORDER AND ORGANIZATION

The next question: where are you ordered and organized most?

Whether you think of yourself as organized or disorganized, you have some areas of order and some areas of disorder in your life. You will spend time organizing the items and areas that are truly most important to you. You will tend to bring order and organization to them. Conversely, you will tend to have chaos and disorder in areas that are low on your list of values.

Look at where you have the greatest degree of order and organization in your life.

- Do you have an organized social calendar?
- Do you have an organized workout schedule?
- Do you have an organized eating or dietary regime?
- Do you have an organized clothes and shoes closet?
- Are your finances organized?
- Do you have an organized business agenda and management routine?
- Do you have an organized cooking arrangement?
- Do you have organized management of your children?

Look at where you display the highest degree of order and organization. Do not lie to yourself and say you don't have such order in your life. Just look for where it is.

Reflect on you daily life and answer these three questions:

Where are you organized and ordered the most?

_____

Where are you organized and ordered the second most?

_____

Where are you organized and ordered the third most?

_____

6. DISCIPLINE

Now we turn to discipline. In what areas are you most disciplined, reliable, and focused? You will be most disciplined in areas of your highest values.

If some goal is important to you, you will be dedicated to achieving it: you won't have to be repeatedly reminded or motivated from the outside. You will be inspired from within.

Look at the areas where you are most disciplined, reliable, and focused—where nobody has to get you up or remind you to do or act.

- Is it your studies?
- Is it your workout routine?
- Is it your social or social media interaction?
- Is it your appearance?
- Is it your dietary or eating regime?
- Is it your business management or activities?
- Is it your family?

Look carefully and be honest with yourself. Answer the three following questions:

Where are you most disciplined, reliable, and focused?

_____

Where are you second most disciplined, reliable, and focused?

_____

Where are you third most disciplined, reliable, and focused?

_____

7. WHAT YOU THINK ABOUT

What do you inwardly think about most? What three subjects most dominate your thoughts?

I am not referring to momentary or transient distractions or self-deprecating thoughts. I am referring to what you most think about that you would love to fulfill and is gradually manifesting in your life.

Your mind will repeatedly focus on the subject that has great meaning for you—whatever is highest on your list of values. You may be momentarily distracted by a phone call or a television program, but your mind will consistently return to the area of highest importance.

The key here is to identify what you are commonly thinking about concerning how you would love your life to be, what you would love to do, or what you would love to have that is coming true. If it is not what you truly think about most, do not write it. If it is not what you would truly love to fulfill in your life, do not write it. If it is not gradually being brought into reality, do not write it.

Make sure the answers to this question reflect the dominant thoughts that are actually and gradually coming true. Do not write down fantasies that are not being realized or not being brought into your reality. Don't write down imperatives, or outer-directed shoulds, ought to's, or supposed to's. Only write down what you specifically think about—about how you would love your life to be—that you are gradually bringing about: those thoughts that are truly showing fruitfulness and are slowly and steadily showing evidence of being brought into your life.

Answer these questions:

What do you inwardly think about the most?

_____

What do you inwardly think about the second most?

_____

What do you inwardly think about the third most?

_____

8. WHAT YOU VISUALIZE

Now we go on to what you visualize. What are you visualizing about how you would love your life to be that shows evidence of coming true? Is it gradually coming true? What you most consistently envision and dream about will be in alignment with what is most important to you.

This vision is to be showing signs of gradually coming true in your life. Do not include subjects you fantasize about that are not coming true—no delusions or unrealistic expectations, only visions about what you would love that are becoming reality.

- Do you dream most about your family life?
- Do you dream most about financial freedom and becoming wealthy?
- Is it traveling the world?

- Is it continually expanding your education and wisdom?
- Is it meeting and socializing with amazing people?
- Is it becoming a leader in your field of expertise?
- Is it leading or managing a great business?

What do you visualize about your future life that you would love to see come true that is gradually, slowly but surely coming true? Write down your three answers.

What do you visualize and then realize most?

_____

What do you visualize and then realize second most?

_____

What do you visualize and then realize third most?

_____

9. SELF-TALK

You talk to yourself about what is most important to you. What do you keep talking to yourself about most that you would love to come true and that is showing evidence of coming true? I do not mean momentary negative self-talk or self-aggrandizement. I mean how you talk to yourself about how you would love your life to be that is showing fruit.

What are the three objectives that you keep talking to yourself about most that you would love to fulfill and they are slowly but surely coming true? Answer these three questions:

What do you internally dialogue with yourself about most?

_____

What do you internally dialogue with yourself about second most?

_____

What do you internally dialogue with yourself about third most?

_____

10. EXTERNAL DIALOGUE

What do you most often want to talk to others about? When you are having conversations, what subject do you keep wanting to bring up? What do you externally dialogue about most?

Like everyone else, you want to share or communicate what is most important to you. If someone discusses a subject that doesn't interest you, you will try to change the conversation to a subject that does, or possibly just withdraw or walk away.

You become an extravert when you talk about what is most important to you. When somebody else talks about it, you come alive. When somebody talks about a subject that is not important to you, you become quiet and introverted, and you want to change the conversation to what is more important to you.

If you go up to somebody and they ask you how your children are, it probably means that their children are important to them. If they ask how your business is doing, business is important. Similarly with other areas, such as relationships or financial investments.

What do you want to bring the conversation to? What do you want to ask questions about and talk about? What are the three subjects you can't wait to discuss?

What do you most talk about in social settings?

What do you talk about second most in social settings?

What do you talk about third most in social settings?

---

11. INSPIRATION

Have a look at your life and ask yourself what inspires you most and what is common to the people that inspire you the most.

- Is it great moments of mastery?
- Is it when you or someone else conquers an amazing challenge or fear?
- Is it achieving a meaningful goal?
- Is it when a great leader, actor, performer, or thinker presents or performs their masterpiece?
- Is it when you hear the meaningful lyrics of an amazing song?
- Is it when you are studying a particular topic and you feel you solved a mystery?

You are generally most inspired in the area of your life that means most to you. If you value your children, you will probably be inspired by their accomplishments. If you value your business, you will probably be inspired by your or others' business achievements. If you love building wealth, you will probably be inspired by having your investments grow against the odds, or by wealthy individuals. If you love learning, you are likely to be inspired by learning new pieces of the puzzle of life or by great scholars or thinkers.

Write down the three actions or subjects that inspire you and/or are common to the people that inspire you the most.

What inspires you most?

_____

What inspires you second most?

_____

What inspires you third most?

_____

12. LONG-TERM GOALS

What are your most persistent and consistent long-term goals that you would love to fulfill, match how you would love your life to be, and are showing evidence of coming true?

What are the three most persistent goals that you have persistently focused on and that you are definitely and gradually bringing into reality?

Do not write down fantasies that you are not acting upon and with which nothing is happening. Write only the ones that you are slowly but surely bringing into your reality. These areas have been dominating your mind and thoughts for a long time, and you keep taking step-by-step actions towards bringing them into reality.

What is your most consistent long-term goal?

_____

What is your second most consistent long-term goal?

_____

What is your third most consistent long-term goal?

---

13. STUDY

What topics of study inspire you most? What do you seek out in bookstores, newsletters, documentaries, and online sources of information? The three answers to these questions will help reveal your highest values.

What do you love to learn about most?

What do you love to learn about second most?

What do you love to learn about third most?

COLOR-CODE YOUR ANSWERS

Once you've entered 3 answers for each of the 13 questions, you'll see among your 39 answers a clearly developed pattern. There is a certain amount of repetition, perhaps even a lot. You may be expressing the same kind of value in different ways, for example, "spending time with people I like," "having a drink with the folks from work," "going out to eat with my friends." If you look closely, you can see patterns emerge.

Go back through the answers. Take colored markers or pencils. Mark all similar answers with the same color. Do that until all your answers are grouped into color categories.

It is possible that you will have two or more categories where the numbers are close or possibly even equal. If so, mark each one by order of what your life truly shows as preference: 1, 2, 3, and so on. Look at what your life truly demonstrates. When you have a choice between the two, which one is predominantly demonstrated?

Next, name each category (color group) of answers according to one of the seven areas of life they show that you value: spiritual, mental, vocational, financial, familial, social, and physical. You may have your top three values in only one of the seven areas, or it may be two or three.

Now rank the categories from the largest to the smallest. You can even calculate the percentages: for example, if you have 13 answers related to vocational or familial, that's 33 percent.

This sequence will give you a clear idea of what you truly value—not what you think you ought to value.

LIFE SUMMARY

Finally, it is helpful to capture what your current values or priorities actually are at the time of doing the value determination. You may go through this process again on another day and come up with results that are slightly or possibly substantially different. (As you accumulate these summaries over time, being able to recap what was going on at each moment will be of immediate later value.) But the repeatedly discovered pattern will most likely continue to emerge.

Write short paragraphs, each of them summarizing what is currently going on in your life in seven basic areas:

1. **Spiritual:** Your meaningful purpose or inspired mission for your life.

2. **Mental:** Creating innovative ideas that contribute to the world and using your mental capacities to the fullest.

3. **Vocational:** Business, career, success, achievement, service.

4. **Financial:** Financial freedom and independence.

5. **Familial:** Family love and intimacy.

6. **Social:** Social influence and leadership.

7. **Physical:** Health, stamina, strength, and well-being.

In any of these areas that you don't empower, others will tend to overpower.

- If you don't empower yourself **spiritually**, you may be told some antiquated geocentric and anthropomorphic dogma that may not be rational or empowering.
- If you don't empower yourself in your **mental** capacities, you'll likely be told what to think.
- If you don't empower yourself in **business**, you'll be told what to do.
- If you don't empower yourself in **finance**, you'll be told what you're worth.
- If you don't empower yourself in **relationships**, you may end up doing what you don't want to do.
- If you don't empower yourself **socially**, you'll be told what propaganda to believe.
- If you don't empower yourself **physically**, you'll be told what drugs to take or organs to remove.

The more areas of your life you don't empower, the more likely you are to feel that you are a victim of your history instead of a master of your destiny. You'll feel that the world is controlling you and that you are living by duty and not by design.

In my opinion, that's not the wisest way to live.

I believe it's wiser to empower all seven areas of your life.

So look at your writing about these seven areas and ask:

- In which of these areas am I empowered and currently further empowering myself?
- In which of these areas am I disempowered and currently allowing myself to be overpowered?
- Are there any areas where I'm just not sure about how empowered I am?

The final step:

List below your current top areas of empowerment.

_____

_____

List below your current top areas of disempowerment.

_____

_____

If you've followed the above directions carefully, you will have a clear idea of your true hierarchy of values. Your major areas of empowerment and disempowerment, advantage and disadvantage, and order and disorder reflect your hierarchy of values.

6

Practical Applications

At this point, we've explored the two major aspects of emotional intelligence: (1) balancing out emotions by seeing both sides of any given trait, action, or inaction; (2) understanding our own true values. We've come far enough in our explorations to see how our discoveries can remedy many common so-called dysfunctions.

Dealing with Anxiety

Many people say that their biggest challenge is feelings of anxiety. Anxiety derives from causes similar to the ones we've already seen. Let's say a little boy one to two years old is sitting in the house, and the mother and father are having a fight. The little boy crawls off to his room, hides underneath the bed, and covers up his ears and eyes to protect himself. He doesn't want to hear mommy and daddy fighting and falls asleep to protect himself from it. He has an associated memory of daddy wearing blue jeans and a white shirt and of mommy wearing a certain dress during the fight.

The next morning, the little boy gets up and sees that mommy and daddy are now calm. Daddy's going to work and mommy's at home.

Mommy soon takes the boy to the grocery store. She is wearing the same dress as last night, and the boy sees a man going down the aisle in blue jeans and a white shirt and with the same color hair as his father. That causes a reaction—a secondary association with the primary event from the night before. We can stack up new associations with primary events that create compounding secondary and even tertiary associated events, which keep reminding us of the first event, bringing up and complicating these reactions.

The little boy, seeing a man walking down the aisle with blue jeans and a white shirt, might have a reaction. He's now associated this man with the event of the night before. He might try to protect mommy or hide behind her to protect himself. If he feels he could fight the man and defend mommy, he'll get in front of mommy. If he wants to flee, he will get behind her.

Then mommy takes the boy down the next aisle and sees a man with blue jeans and the same color hair as daddy, but this time wearing a yellow shirt. Another association is made.

We can keep adding and compounding associations. All we need is one of those items from the initial event to trigger a reaction, and the new secondary or tertiary associations compound the reaction further. After a while, hundreds of associations can trigger reminders of the original traumatic event. As long as we have that initial painful association stored in our mind, secondary and tertiary compoundings of events can trigger that response.

Anxiety is the accumulation of these secondary and tertiary compoundings. After a while, we don't even know why we're having an anxiety attack; still, we feel we're being attacked, unconscious of all the different stimuli that are triggering it. If you don't go back to that original event, neutralize it, find the blessings on the other side, and see how it's served you and those involved, it will probably keep running your life until you do.

In the Breakthrough Experience, I work with people with so-called anxiety disorders. Sometimes we have to peel the associations off like layers of an onion, going back one by one and neutralizing them. At other times, it's possible to use regression to go to the original so-called trauma at once and neutralize it so that the whole complex collapses and dissolves.

In short, anxiety is a compounding of associations added to an original painful event that was perceived to have had more drawbacks than benefits. Any stimuli that you perceive that remind you of this event, even in the subtlest ways, can cause an anxiety or avoidance reaction to protect you from reexperiencing that initial experience. You're protecting yourself from this event because you have chosen to see its drawbacks without seeing its blessings. You remain conscious of the downsides and unconscious of the upsides. The anxiety dissolves away once we balance the initial event with an equal amount of upsides to balance the downsides.

Emotions are imbalanced perspectives. Knowing how to ask the right questions to bring them back into balance is the art and the science of mastery. We're no longer sitting in the plateaus of anxieties, holding ourselves back from life. Once we master the skill of balancing our perceptions, we elevate our degree of emotional intelligence.

Medication

Many people today are using medication to treat depression and anxiety. Let me give my own perspective on this issue.

If a hungry tiger was suddenly let into your room, about to leap across the floor towards you with a salivating mouth and a sharp set of fangs and teeth, you would become alarmed, aware that you could be eaten, and your brain chemistry would become suddenly imbalanced as a result of your amygdala's survival response.

If we stopped it right before it was about to eat your head and we checked the biochemistry in your blood and brain, we would find that your endorphin, enkephalin, serotonin, dopamine, estrogen, vasopressin, and oxytocin levels would all be immediately depressed, while their complementary opposite counterneurotransmitters—testosterone, osteocalcin, adrenaline, noradrenaline, cortisol, histamine, and substance P—would be simultaneously elevated.

The ratio of your negative to positive perceptions would immediately impact and determine the ratio of your neurotransmitters and neurohormones. Your brain chemistry does not just randomly become imbalanced: it requires real or imagined stimuli and previously stored associations to initiate such a response.

If you then suddenly discovered that the tiger's name was Tony the Tiger, the character from your childhood breakfast cereal Frosted Flakes, and that he wanted to give you a giant hug and tell you, "You're *grrrreat!*" and you've been wanting to meet him since you were a child, your neurochemistry would immediately change again: it would flop in the opposite direction within milliseconds. The previous neurochemicals would decline and the new, opposite neurochemicals would emerge: suddenly dopamine, serotonin, enkephalins, endorphins, estrogen, oxytocin, and vasopressin would rise.

Any imbalanced perceptions stored in your subconscious mind, can, when joined with new alarming stimuli, result in the so-called imbalanced chemistries found in your brain.

Your brain has many self-governing, homeostatic, negative feedback systems that constantly attempt to return any temporarily imbalanced neurochemistry back into balance. But the memory storage of previously polarized emotions and their resultant impulses and instincts prolong such neurochemical imbalances. Many psychological and physiological illnesses can emerge from chronically stored neurochemical imbalances and their associated emotions.

Medical psychiatry often listens briefly to your story, possibly analyzes your brain and blood chemistries and says, "You have a biochemical imbalance; let's balance it with chemical drugs." That's fine. I'm not saying that there's not a place for it, but I would much rather teach people how to take command of their lives than become dependent on a drug.

I've seen too many cases where people end up on medication when they may just not need to. They may not, if they learn the questions that equilibrate their mind and reclaim their power. I would say that chemistry and drugs are a secondary, not a primary approach. I prefer to help people reclaim their power back, not take it away. Self-mastery and high emotional intelligence is seldom if ever an outer drug dependent state. The inner pharmaceutical dispensary in your brain is far more effective in most cases than the one on the outer street corner.

Taking Events Personally

A lot of people also say that they take events too personally: their feelings are hurt and they're not able to move past the perceived issue. Here is how I often approach this matter.

If somebody attacks and criticizes you, you're probably going to react unless you've taken the time to balance your perception of the criticisms you've had in the past. If you've never taken the time to do that, you're, again, going to store those imbalances in your subconscious mind. You're going to be vulnerable and react. Whenever someone reminds you of that original traumatic event, you're going to withdraw.

In the Breakthrough Experience, I deal with this imbalance in two ways. First, I find and show you where, at the exact moment of the criticism, somebody else was honoring, respecting, and praising you. I would do this to help you become aware of both sides of the event you had perceived, which is actually helping you become whole and authentic.

Second, you also want to look at the benefit of this criticism. Could the other individual, in that moment, actually be teaching you how to communicate more effectively? Could it be that you're cocky and need to be humbled a bit? Could it be that you're not respecting them, you're projecting your expectations on them and not honoring their values? It could be that they're just having a challenging day: they're just projecting their frustrations onto you, and it has nothing to do with you as an individual. In any case, unless you clear out past experiences, you will probably react. That's why it's wise to neutralize your subconsciously stored memories from previous times: it will give you a higher probability of preventing overreactions in the future.

But let's say you do initially react to criticism. What can you do now? You can stop and ask yourself some questions. (Again, the quality of your life is based upon the quality of the questions you ask and answer for yourself.) First of all, you can ask, where have I done that same behavior? Where have I criticized and attacked and rejected somebody? If you see that you're doing exactly what they have been doing to the same degree, quantitatively and qualitatively, you're unlikely to further react. The second question is, how does this criticism serve you? Once you discover that the criticism has exactly as many benefits as drawbacks, you no longer perceive a wound. If you ask a new set of questions, you're going to have a different response.

If you're addicted to praise, criticism is going to hurt, and you're going to take it very personally. In these cases, you're usually attributing false power to the other individual. You're assuming their opinion is more important than yours. You've got a wound in the past that you haven't neutralized. Any emotionally charged event you have not loved will run your life until you love or balance it.

That's why I developed the Demartini Method. Its purpose is to ask those questions and clear those subconscious imbalances. I have yet to see any imbalances that can't be neutralized by asking the right questions and being held accountable for answering them completely.

Depression

Many people today are concerned about or claiming to be experiencing and "suffering" from depression. Here is how I see it: depression is a comparison of your current reality to a fantasy or an unrealistic expectation you keep holding on to. I've sometimes been challenged and even attacked by people that come up to me and say, "I have depression; I have a biochemical imbalance." Their pharmaceutical minded and trained psychiatrists, and possibly media advertising, have gotten embedded into their heads and convinced them that this is the case. But I rarely see a true deficiency of drugs in those that claim to be depressed.

"Really?" I reply to such people. "Do you mind if I take you through a simple questioning process and see if there is some other reason that's more likely to be true?" I have yet to find one case for which I can't find some underlying reasons behind the depression, sorrow, or grief.

Your current reality is actually balanced. It is filled with paired perceptual opposites. But through your perceptions, you believed it is imbalanced. You are conscious of some portions of your current reality and unconscious of other portions. You unknowingly have false positive and false negative distortions of your whole current reality. This is partly because you're comparing it to what you think it "ought to" be according to an unrealistic expectation, fantasy, or somebody else's expectations or values. Of course you're going to be depressed.

Depression is feedback to let you know you don't have the strategies to meet your expectations, which probably aren't in line with your own highest values anyway. Your expectations are more likely an internalized version of somebody else's expectations or fantasies, which are often not even feasible. I think it's disrespectful to people to tell them they have a correlated chemical imbalance when more often the real truth is that they can have the power to change their own lives without having to depend on a drug. Dissolving the unrealistic expectations or fantasies and grounding them and discovering the hidden benefits of the current reality can liberate feelings of depression. Changing expectations and perceptions and their corresponding and correlating neurochemistry can give individuals their power back. Managing and objectivizing such expectations and their resulting emotions is what emotional intelligence is all about.

I know that some people are not willing to be accountable for their expectations or perceptions: they're not willing to grow, they're not willing to be masters of life, and they'll submit to an alternative path. I'm glad that the pharmaceutical path is there: it serves people that may not be willing to master their perceptions, decisions, and actions. But if you want to master your life, begin to ask wise and meaningful questions to break down the illusions that are leading to these distracting or depressing emotional feelings.

Emotions versus Feelings

Polarized emotions result from imbalanced perceptions or perspectives. They're letting you know what questions to ask in order to balance them. Most people think that all feelings are emotions, but I define these two concepts differently. *Emotions* are polarized, imbalanced perspectives and the feelings associated with them, which can be either positive or negative: joy, sorrow, happiness, sadness, attraction, repulsion, like, dislike, infatuation, resentment, admiration, contempt, mania, depression. Polarized emotions initiate survival-based seeking impulses and avoiding instincts.

There are also six genuine and integrated *feelings*, which are not polarized emotions. I call them *transcendental feelings*: true gratitude, true love, true inspiration, true enthusiasm, true certainty, and true presence. They spontaneously emerge when you awaken to the balanced and hidden order within your apparent chaos and you become fully conscious (more than just conscious and unconscious). In my Breakthrough Experience, I show people how to dissolve the subconscious baggage they've been unnecessarily carrying around and transform it into those genuine transcendental or superconscious feelings. These are empowering; these are masterful.

I believe that you are capable of understanding these distinctions and learning how to neutralize your emotional imbalances—which enhances your emotional intelligence. If you do, you will seldom if ever have any "legitimate" reason to wallow in emotional states, run stories, or go to your therapist all the time (I call it *running your racket*). It's wiser to ask yourself questions, balance out your perceptions, dissipate your polarized emotions, and synthesize your feelings into ones of gratitude, love, certainty, presence, inspiration and enthusiasm. These are the transcendental feelings that empower people.

Crying

Some people claim that one of their challenges in balancing their emotions is that they can come to tears or cry quite easily. I've sometimes been asked to explain the purpose of crying and what someone can do to address the propensity to cry when challenged.

Some species of animals, such as elephants, cry. But with humans, I don't think the experts have ever pinned down a sole and absolute reason for crying. Nevertheless, we can make some general statements about it.

Crying basically comes in three types. First, there's joy: you're so happy that a tear comes to your eye. Second, you can have tears when you're sorrowful and depressed. Third, you can have tears when you're inspired and see the hidden order in life—the divine master plan, the real hidden order of your universe. All three types have different chemistries.

There are a number of reasons for sorrowful tears. Babies cry as a primitive way of communicating. Mothers know their babies' cries and what they're trying to communicate. This type usually fades out around the ages of three to five.

Crying could also be a strategy: when you feel hurt or injured, you may use it as a default mechanism to change the chemistry in the brain. When you cry, it changes your levels of ACTH (which is a hormone) and endorphin; it's a way of resetting the emotional center—like shivering when you are cold.

This function is like the capacitor in electronics: a device that stores energy by accumulating electric charges on two close surfaces, such as plates, which are insulated from each other. If the voltage is strong enough, electricity is discharged across the plates. Similarly, if you have a big enough emotion, it discharges and resets the level of tension. Some people feel at least a temporary relief when they cry. Yet if they don't dissolve their emotionally imbalanced perspectives, the tension is going to build up again, and they're probably going to cry again.

Another purpose for tears: research has shown that if an individual cries, they generate an altruistic response, stopping the attacker. In that case, crying may work as a kind of strategy. Sometimes it's a way of getting sympathy or empathy; sometimes it's a means to accomplish an end.

Crying can also diffuse conflict. If the parents are fighting, the children will cry and stop the conflict.

Crying can be a useful tool for rebalancing chemistries when you don't have a way of balancing them cognitively. But I believe that it's much wiser to balance out your perceptions by using your forebrain than it is to use primitive animal reactions and unconscious strategies (which underlie many illnesses). It's wiser and more meaningful to become conscious of the unconscious and balance out the perceptions so you don't feel you have to cry out of polarized emotions but instead awaken a greater awareness of the hidden order and have a tear of gratitude and inspiration from the eureka moment of awe.

Sometimes people come to the Breakthrough Experience with stories of their so-called traumatic events. They want to run their racket, and they're crying. I ask some Demartini Method questions to balance out the perceived trauma and bring them back in touch with a balanced reality, or actuality. The second they're back in balance, the sorrowful wound-based crying stops, and they're grateful. Then they have authenticity-confirming tears of gratitude, not tears of sorrow.

As Ralph Waldo Emerson has stated it, "We come to them who weep foolishly and sit down and cry for company, instead of imparting to them truth and health in rough electric shocks putting them once more in communication with the reason of their soul."

Emotions can be neutralized, reset, or rebalanced by asking the right questions. Your intuition is constantly attempting to question your consciousness in order to help you see the other side of the full conscious equation—your unconscious. If you're infatuated, you're conscious to the upsides but blind, ignorant, or unconscious to the downsides of what you're infatuated with. Conversely, if you're resentful, you're conscious of the downsides and unconscious of the upsides. Your intuition is trying to make you aware of the other, unconscious side, which you're ignoring. If you let your intuition guide you, it will bring you back into full conscious balance; the polarized emotions will go away, and the synthesized feelings of love and gratitude will come back. Tears of sorrow will turn into tears of gratitude and inspiration. To me, that is healing. That's promoting wellness, not illness.

I created the Demartini Method and the Breakthrough Experience because I want people to know how to dissolve their emotional charges instead of constantly and cyclically building them up and discharging them. You don't want to get caught in a loop, discharging tension with crying, like a little child, instead of dissolving the charge, balancing the equation, and having mastery over life. That's much wiser, more emotionally intelligent, and more wellness-promoting, in my opinion.

Negative Self-Talk

Many people say their biggest challenge is negative self-talk, self-depreciation, or self-sabotage. I love attacking this illusion of sabotage and negative self-talk.

What I'm about to say may shock you: as long as you're addicted to praise and you like to be puffed up and proud of yourself, your internal thermostat, homeostat, or "psychostat" *has to* beat you up with negative self-talk to return you to your true and authentic self.

Usually, when I teach the Breakthrough Experience, I pick somebody out of the audience and say, "You're always nice; you're never mean. You're always kind; you're never cruel. You're always positive, never negative. You're always generous, never stingy. You're always peaceful, never wrathful. You're always considerate, never inconsiderate. Isn't that true?"

The individual will usually reply saying, "No, not really."

Then I go on: "No, no. Let me redo that. You're always mean; you're never nice. You're always cruel; you're never kind. You're always negative, you're never positive. You're always wrathful, never peaceful. You're always taking; you're never giving. You're always inconsiderate; you're never considerate. Would you believe that?"

"No."

Then I say, "Would you believe that sometimes you're nice; sometimes you're mean? Sometimes you're kind; sometimes you're cruel. Sometimes you build yourself up; sometimes you beat yourself up. Sometimes you're generous; sometimes you're stingy. Sometimes you're peaceful; sometimes you're wrathful. Sometimes you're positive; sometimes you're negative. Would you believe that?"

"Yes," they'll say.

We have a built-in intuitive thermostat that knows the more objective truth: we're both sides at once. For the first two declarations, I stated that their responses were uncertain, but for the final declaration of both-sidedness, they were certain. You intuitively know you are two-sided, not one-sided. But you may lose sight of this once you have skewed your perceptual reality.

As long as we're addicted to looking for a one-sided magnetic outcome, the other side of the magnet is going to keep smacking us. As long as we're addicted to and pleasured by admiration and praise, we're going to be hurt by rejection and criticism. As long as we're addicted to pride, we're going to be vulnerable to and frightened by shame. Our built-in thermostat brings in negative self-talk when we're addicted to positive self-talk. Addiction to positive self-talk breeds negative self-talk. It is a version of the moral licensing effect to keep us centered and authentic. We know innately that we are both hero and villain, saint and sinner, and all other pairs of behavioral opposites. If we had a drone watching over us all day for weeks on end, we could easily take footage of the two sides of our double-sided nature and behavior.

I don't try to put only positive self-talk into the brain, as I once did when I was younger and more gullible; I simply put *balanced* talk in the brain. I've been doing this for many years, and I'm certain that this balanced orientation is much more grounded, productive, and real.

A goal that's one-sided, that's not balanced, that doesn't have the downsides, is not a real goal or objective; it's a fantasy. As soon as you create an unrealistic expectation for a one-sided outcome, negative self-talk, self-deprecation, anxiety and doubts are automatically designed to come into your mind to show you both sides. When the negative self-talk and the positive self-talk have been balanced, you will be able to set a real, balanced goal, or objective and more effectively achieve.

Nobody's one-sided. When an individual can finally embrace both sides of their life, they can love themselves. You don't need to get rid of half of your life to love yourself. You don't need to get rid of half of anybody else to love them. The real truth is, you're both hero and villain. You're saint and sinner. Until you can embrace both sides of yourself, don't expect to master your life. If you're trying to get rid of half of yourself, you won't fully empower yourself. I don't try to get rid of one half; I simply teach people about the importance of integrating the two and having mastery. This is more emotionally intelligent.

I've had people that have had emotional or so-called allergic reactions to food, to certain types of people and certain types of behaviors. I've identified what associations trigger those reactions and where and when they are. I've peeled the onion back through its many layers, going through each one of those episodes when the reaction occurred and neutralized it with the Demartini Method.

Another approach I have used is to regress the individual to the earliest experience, neutralize it, and watch the whole series of secondary and tertiary associations tumble down in a domino effect. The next time somebody comes along and does something that previously irritated the individual, they no longer psychologically or physiologically react.

Almost every week in the Breakthrough Experience, people have said that they and some family member have been fighting. "We've almost gone at each other's throats," they tell me. We go in, find the past triggers, and neutralize them. Later they report that the next time they saw that family member, they didn't react anymore.

"They don't push my buttons," they tell me.

"Because you dissolved the imbalanced triggering button," I reply.

A button is any experience in your life that you never took the time to balance; it's still stored in your subconscious mind. Some women come to me and say, "I keep getting hooked by the same kind of guy." I know one woman who married five men named Michael who were alcoholics. Individuals like her are drawn to some infatuation but end up drawing in the opposite. Each individual has each of the many human behaviors and its opposite. They are being hooked over and over again by highly polarized positives and negatives. The repercussions of this process are often frustrating until you discover their message and neutralize the hooks.

If you can see an emotional reaction, stop. Use that feedback to let you know what you haven't loved and haven't balanced. Use the Demartini Method and balance the reaction. Let's clear it out. From then on, you'll notice that when those people behave in ways you previously found irritating, they don't run you anymore. You run you and you appreciate them for waking you up to what you had not loved.

Anything that you don't neutralize is going to run your life until you neutralize it. Anything you don't love and appreciate is going to run your life until you love and appreciate it. Anything you haven't loved and appreciated is baggage. Anything you have loved, appreciated, and balanced in your life is fuel. If you want to fuel your life, clear the baggage.

Positive Emotions?

I've sometimes been asked what role positive emotions play in life. The answer is simply they act as feedback responses to what you have not yet perceptually balanced and loved and opportunities to love them. Both positive and negative emotions alone reflect an imbalanced state. As we've seen, I draw a contrast between emotions—which reflect imbalances—and true balanced feelings, which are integrated and transcendent.

If you're infatuated with somebody and you've put them on a pedestal, thinking they have something you don't, you'll seek them like prey; figuratively speaking, you want to eat them. Similarly, if you resent somebody, conscious only of the negatives you see in them, you now have resentment. Both of those two polarities initiate emotions involving seeking or avoidance. Any emotion that is experienced that has never been brought back into balance will stay in your subconscious mind indefinitely. If you are expressing a positive emotion, you are simultaneously consciously suppressing or unconsciously repressing its negative counterpart.

Some people have emotional buttons from fifty years ago. I've known individuals that have had emotional charges over something their parents did when they were two years old. Now they're sixty, and they're still having reactions. Or someone is still reacting to an affair that occurred thirty-five years ago. Anything that you haven't balanced in your mind is stored in the subconscious mind; it keeps coming up and reverberates. During both dreams and daily life, the brain is intuitively trying to balance these perceived events and their accompanying emotions. Although this does occasionally happen, many people are stuck in reverberating cycles, particularly if the emotion is compounded by secondary and tertiary stimuli. The wisest course is to identify those moments, go into them, and ask the questions that neutralize them. Take the subconscious information, balance it out, and bring it into the superconscious state. When you can see the balance in the situation, you don't react, and you become self-governed.

The executive center in your brain has the capacity to overrule your more emotionally urgent amygdala. Whenever you're living by high-priority actions and balancing out your perceptions more objectively, you're training your brain to act instead of react. I suggest finding those previously reactive moments, going back to the exact original moment and neutralizing it. Go in and ask the questions: If you saw that somebody was criticizing you, ask, who was praising me? Where have I behaved in the same way myself? What was the benefit of it? Own and neutralize it equally, 100 percent. Give yourself permission to elevate your self-governing emotional intelligence.

Every event has both sides, so if you can balance out your perceptions and become aware of both sides at once simultaneously, it has no power over you. Until you do, it's going to keep running your life. You can't escape what you haven't loved. Once you love it, you're free, and you're thankful for the experience, because you've grown from it.

Every time you complete this process, you go to the next illusive set of emotions that can be neutralized. Whenever you clear a set of emotions and become empowered, you automatically go to the next set or pair of emotion you haven't cleared, and you get to work on that. Your emotions are letting you know what you haven't had the opportunity to love and giving you an opportunity to love again.

I'm occasionally asked about the best way to express emotions. I avoid using moral language, saying a particular choice is right or wrong. That's not the way I would describe it. I would just say that every human being is going to have a seeking or avoiding emotional reaction to anything they perceive in an imbalanced way. You can keep running the same story over and over and compounding it, and it will keep running your life. Or you can use those emotional experiences as stimuli to ask new sets of questions, balance out your perceptions, broaden your mind, and open your heart. Ask the questions that your intuition is constantly attempting to prompt in your mind: the questions that bring it back into balance. Then you're using your emotions wisely.

That is exactly what emotional intelligence is about: as I said at the very beginning of this book, it is having governance over your perceptions, decisions, and actions. You do this by asking questions that balance your perceptions and their resultant emotions. When you know you've balanced them, you'll have gratitude, you'll have love, and you'll feel inspired. You'll feel enthused about how this illusive emotion has served you, you'll be certain about where you're going, and you'll be present. You will awaken to the hidden order and meaning of the perceived event. You won't be sitting there with subconsciously stored and distorted memories and imaginations. These more meaningful and inspiring responses confirm that you've used your emotions wisely as feedback: you've asked the questions that prompt your mind to equilibrate and move through them, breaking through into a new plateau and going on to the next set of illusive emotions. Then you do it again. It's lovely. You are not here to get rid of, or even repress or suppress your emotions; You are here to use them wisely, to do something extraordinary with your life. Your philias and phobias are there to teach you what you have yet to love and offer you a reminder that it is time to begin to love.

Fear

Many people have asked what to do about fear. Your phobias, or fears, are a result of your philias or fantasies. In other words, your philias breed your phobias, your fantasies breed your nightmares. Now let me explain what that means.

Let's say that you're single and you see a handsome man or beautiful woman. You're enamored of them, so you subjectively perceive that they display or demonstrate many more positives than negatives, and you're completely blinded by infatuation. You get goo-goo eyes, and you think, "Oh, my God! This is the one. We're soulmates."

As a result of this line of thinking, you're going to automatically fear the loss of that individual. The second you have an infatuation, a philia, you simultaneously fear the loss of the one you're infatuated with, or have a phobia.

On the other side, let's say you resent somebody: you think, "I don't even want to see them again." You're resentful and angry: you perceive all the negatives and don't perceive any positives. Now you have a fear or phobia of this individual coming to you and a fantasy or philia of them being avoided or staying away.

You fear the loss of that which you are infatuated with. You fear the gain of that which you resent. You fantasize about the gain of that which you are infatuated with. You fantasize about the loss of that which you resent. Philias and phobias are inseparable. They're in each emotionally charged moment and each case, paired. They're entangled like two poles of a magnet. The philia is the positive pole; the phobia is the negative pole.

Philia is an assumption that you will experience more positives than negatives in the future; phobia is an assumption that you will experience more negatives than positives. Both are imbalanced perspectives. As long as we have imbalanced perceptions, are functioning from our subcortical amygdala, trying to seek pleasure and avoid pain in a world that simultaneously has a balance, we're going to have a life ridden with philic fantasies and phobic nightmares much of the time.

That's why living by your highest priorities or values and awakening your executive center is so important: it gives you more objective goals that are balanced with foresight, mitigating risk. You set real goals or objectives that are reasonable in real time, and you achieve them. That's where and when you get the most accomplishment. Great achievements don't come by immediate gratifying impulses; they come from moments of foresight, planning, and visualizing from within your executive center. Your emotional intelligence is designed to help you fulfill your life.

Practical Balancing

If you want to know the practical steps you can take today to bring about a greater level of emotional intelligence or balance to your mind, first go to the exact moment where and when you perceive yourself displaying or demonstrating one of these traits, actions, or inactions that have initiated your polarized emotions, either towards yourself or towards others, and become present. It is in that present moment when the conscious and unconscious portions of your mind began to separate and your subjective bias or judgment emerged. It is also at this moment when they can be reintegrated.

Many say, "I have a fear of the unknown." In my many years of studying human behavior, I've not seen anybody that has fear of the unknown. Not once. I think it's a false construct. What we actually have is fear of the content that we're storing in our mind in that moment that we're imagining about to occur. That is in each case knowable, because it's right there in the content of your mind in that moment. You can't have fear of the unknown, but you can have fear of the precise content that you presently have in your mind.

So I suggest going to the moment where and when you've displayed or demonstrated the particular behavior that you're judging in yourself. Narrow it down and identify it. I assure you there is no emotion that is not merely an imbalanced perspective. It's going to be either overpositive or overnegative, but identify it. Once you do this, there's a series of questions you can ask, which I outline as the Demartini Method in the Breakthrough Experience.

For our purposes here, first you ask what specifically are you doing or not doing that you are judging yourself for. If you're judging or criticizing yourself, it's because you're expecting yourself to be doing something different than you just did. That expectation is more often the result of a one-sided unrealistic expectation or fantasy, which is not going to be realized: in fact, you have a built-in thermostat, homeostat, or "psychostat" to make sure that it's not going to happen. Alternatively, you're probably expecting yourself to live outside your own set of values and in somebody else's. But you can't sustainably live this way, because every decision you make is based on your own hierarchy of values: your view of whatever will give you a greater advantage over disadvantage, a greater reward over risk. If you're expecting to consistently live outside your highest values or expect to get one-sided outcomes, you're going to beat yourself up and live with philias and phobias or fantasies and nightmares. You're going to live in or with a self-defeating or sabotaging perspective. But this is not actually sabotage; it's a way of giving yourself feedback to let you know you've got an imbalanced perspective and are attempting to live inauthentically. If you're angry at somebody else, you go and find out how you're expecting them to live in your values and outside their own. You're somehow expecting them to be one-sided, which is an unrealistic expectation. There are no cases in which the individual is beating up either themselves or someone else without having an unrealistic expectation. That's why we have those emotions: they're letting you know that this is going on. That's why your polarized emotion is also your friend, if you know how to ask questions to neutralize it and turn it to your advantage. Using your emotions as a feedback is a sign of having high emotional intelligence.

All you can ever expect anybody to do is live according to their own highest values. They're not committed to you. They're committed to the fulfillment of their own highest values. Every decision they make is based on what they believe will give them the greatest advantage over disadvantage to what they value most in that moment.

So we first identify what the judgment and resultant emotion is, and then we ask how it is related to you: are you judging yourself, or are you judging somebody else? Then we find out the unrealistic expectation that's initiating the emotion and the consequent imbalance. Then we ask, what specifically is the trait, action, or inaction that you're most upset about?

If this trait, action, or inaction involves another individual, you identify where and when you yourself have displayed that same trait and who's seen you do it, until you own it 100 percent. Thereby you calm down some of that judgment-based emotion.

Then you ask, how does this specific trait, action or inaction serve you? Every trait and action somehow serves, or it would have gone extinct. So how is it a service to you? We think that somehow there are "bad" events, but that really isn't totally true: they're just events, and it's not what they've done; it's how we perceived them. We ask how this trait helps us instead of how it hinders us. We can turn it and see the other side (because every event has two sides). Then you find out at that moment who's doing the opposite. You'll find out that this individual is playing in the center of a pair of opposites, and you may be addicted to one, and therefore attracting this other complementary opposite one to break your addiction.

This series of questions enables people to neutralize an emotion; get it back into balance; turn it into gratitude, love, inspiration, enthusiasm, certainty and presence; and say that whatever just happened was *on* the way, not *in* the way.

Now the individual is empowered rather than disempowered and futilely running their racket. Too often I see people running the same story and expecting a different outcome. Stop the story, ask equilibrating questions, and get your intuition to help you neutralize it. Get back to appreciation and love. Express your true love, which is a synthesized, transcendental feeling, not a polarized emotion.

The Demartini Method is a culmination of decades of research, contemplation, and clinical application. I didn't originally call it the Demartini Method; I called it the Quantum Collapse Process. It was based on quantum physics. When I was eighteen years old, with the help of dictionaries and encyclopedias, I read Paul Dirac's 1947 textbook *The Principles of Quantum Mechanics*: he talked about particles and antiparticles joining together to make gamma photons of light. I wondered if you could take the positive and negative emotions of a human being and merge them together at the same time to make enlightenment. This metaphor turned out to be more insightful, practical, and meaningful than initially imagined.

Basically, your brain is doing everything it can to try to equilibrate the lopsided perceptions that you are storing in your subconscious mind or subcortical brain. The Demartini Method is a series of concise questions to help an individual identify any emotion that is limiting their achievements and holding them in bondage. Then they ask the questions that equilibrate their mind and liberate them. At that point, they can move forward to the next lesson, the next illusion. We go from one illusion to another in our life, to the next set of polar emotions, at which point we use the method again. It's not a process you're done with once and for all. Sometimes people ask me, "Once I do this exercise, will I never have another emotion in my life?"

"No," I reply. "That's delusional. You're going to have your buttons pushed throughout your life. I certainly do."

The next time a polarized emotion arises, I pull out the tool, break through the emotion, and go on to our next one. If you're stuck in the same emotions, you're stagnant. If you use those emotions, learn what they're offering as feedback, know how to ask the right questions, proceed to a synthesized transcendent feeling, and go on to the next set of illusions and emotions, then you're using them wisely. You're using your emotions as a feedback mechanism to guide you to do something extraordinary. Your developing your emotional intelligence.

In the Breakthrough Experience, I teach people how to do or apply the Demartini Method. I guide and nudge them through the trials and tribulations of dissolving emotional baggage that they've stored in their subconscious mind. I don't care what it is: the issue may involve relationships, sex, health, business, finances, or social relations—practically everything that could be weighing the individual down emotionally. You ask the specific questions, answer them methodically and honestly, and dissolve the emotion until you reach the point where you can just spontaneously say, thank you. There's nothing your mortal body can experience that your immortal soul can't love. The soul is the state of unconditional love that you can have for anything that you've experienced.

People say, "I'm skeptical of that."

"I understand; that is fine," I reply. "But just come and do it. Then you'll see how certain I am about this process I've been developing, and you'll experience the results." I have not had anyone do the method thoroughly and to completion without experiencing this outcome.

This is a reproducible and methodical science of taking emotional baggage and turning it into fuel so that you're liberated instead of being weighed down. Your emotions are your friends if you are conscious or use them wisely as feedback, but they can weigh you down and hold you back if you don't.

As I've said, the Demartini Method is a duplicable science. If an individual follows and completes it, I can guarantee the results. Of course, if the individual dodges the process and doesn't want to do the introspective work, I can't do anything about that; I can't force them to do it. But if they follow this process, I guarantee they're going to get an eye and heart opening, and a meaningful result. They're going to take anything about which they're initially distraught and ultimately be able to say thank you for it. Anything you can't say thank you for is baggage. I show you how to dissolve the baggage. Again, there is nothing your mortal physical body can experience that your authentic being, or immortal soul cannot transcend.

The Breakthrough Experience is about helping people identify what they value most and what inspires them most. They learn how to prioritize their lives, break through and transcend distraction and subordination to conscious or unconscious outer authorities, and develop their true inner authority. Finally, they are able to set more inspiring and meaningful goals that align congruently with their own highest values.

The Demartini Method can be used to empower all seven areas of your life. I show people how to wake up their genius. If they know that whatever they're studying is linked to what they value most, the brain comes online, and they empower their attention and retention, and in some cases even develop photographic minds. If they can link their job duties to what they value most, they can empower themselves at work and be inspired by it. Or they will have the courage to move on and become entrepreneurs. I show them how their values can make a difference in their finances, because the hierarchy of your values dictates your financial destiny.

By asking questions that equilibrate our brains, liberate us from our subjective biases, and allow us to get more objective, we get to the truth. We realize that there's nobody worth putting on pedestals or in pits, but everybody's worth putting in our hearts. Yes, both the so-called heroes and the villains.

Practical Emotional Intelligence

To speak about practical emotional intelligence, you're interacting with your environment, and as you do, your hierarchy of values is interpreting and responding to it. The thalamus of your brain has a gating mechanism that filters your sensory perceptions and discerns which ones to include and exclude, and to send to the cortical or subcortical areas of your brain. These determinations are made according to your hierarchy of values. Consequently, our hierarchy of values, our set of life priorities, filters our reality. We exclude and include different sensory impressions with what I call *attention surplus* and *attention deficit* respectively. We do this automatically according to what we think will give us the greatest advantage over disadvantage. Every action, every decision, every perception is part of a strategy to accomplish what we think and feel is most important to us.

If that's the case, learning the art of perceiving, deciding, and acting according to our highest values and managing our responses to the environment is the key to mastering life.

When you meet somebody, you have two processes occurring in your brain. Your peripheral sensory receptors—

sight, sound, smell, taste, touch—take in information. (Actually you're using over a hundred different external and internal senses to pick up information, although you may not be aware of it.) As these sense impressions come to the brain, they trigger subconscious emotional experiences from the past, which were polarized and judged as supportive or challenging, pleasureful or painful, seeking or avoiding stimuli. These patterns are imposed on the raw new sense data, structuring your perceptions. As a result, your perception is tainted by your hierarchy of values and the imbalanced experiences that you stored in the past. Anything you perceived as more pleasurable than painful or more attractive than repulsive was stored as an impulse *towards*. Impressions of the opposite kind, which you've associated with pain or challenge, generate an impulse to *avoid*.

It's a system of prey and predator, seek and avoid, impulse and instinct. Our experiences and memories—we'll call them episodic memories—are imposed on the new information coming in through our receptors, and the two join together as associations, often as first percepts and then concepts. This entire scale of receptivity, and perceptivity has emotional overlays. Indeed the emotions are nothing but the ratios of those perceptions. If, for a particular stimulus, you have a ratio of five positive perceptions to twenty negatives, you will have an instinct to avoid it. If you have a ratio of ten positives and one negative, you're going to have a strong impulse to seek it. Because these associations are stored in the survival based, animal area of the brain—the subcortical region—they'll fire off rapidly;

after all, quick responses are necessary for survival. These neurons fire off before you can think. If you don't have any governance over those impulses, they can run you into emotional dysregulation. You overreact, having extreme emotional responses to external stimuli and this represents a lower state of emotional intelligence.

You've seen this occur. You've seen people overreact to trivial matters, having no governance over their impulses, which fire with an emotional response before they can think. If this happens, you react, often in ways not previously intended. Afterward you can sometimes judge yourself for that reaction, because you've been subordinated to a social ideal about how you're supposed to be, which in most cases is merely moral hypocrisy. In any event, these new emotions are stacked on top of previous emotions.

Those emotions are based not only on previous experiences but on subordination to outside ideals and norms that you believe you're supposed to live by, often regardless of your own true highest values and objectives. All of those are woven together into an experience when you perceive. If you are functioning through this lower, emotional part of the brain, you will respond as if to an emergency and will often overreact.

You can also respond from the higher, more advanced cortical part of the brain, which exercises governance: the *executive center*. An individual with more moderate, more neutral, and more balanced ratios of perceptions awakens the forebrain and gets the executive center going, which then uses glutamate, which is a stimulatory transmitter, and

GABA, which is an inhibitory one, and regulates those lower subcortically driven emotions of impulse and instinct.

We've covered a lot of ground in this chapter, including issues that seem highly challenging that affect hundreds of millions of individuals globally, such as anxiety and depression. We've shown that they can all be transformed by an honest and fearless inquiry in which we ask questions about our past and see how every event, action, and quality—whether we initially label them as "good" or "bad"—is balanced by its exact counterpart. To the extent that we understand and practice this broader and more balanced awareness, we can attain not only mental wholeness and well-being, but true wisdom. This empowers our emotional intelligence.

7

The Wisdom of the Ages

For thousands of years, humans have desired to master their lives: to move beyond a survival state towards a thrival state and govern both their themselves and the environment around them. Throughout this time, some individuals, called wise men and women, or simply wise individuals, have probed deeply into those mysteries and recorded what they learned. For the past five decades, I have studied this perennial wisdom, which has been flowing for the thousands of years since the beginning of recorded history. It has been centered around some very similar messages.

Ego, Id, and Superego

There has been a great deal of confusion about the term *ego*, which comes from the Latin *ego*, meaning *I* or *self*. One of the most influential discussions of this concept is that of the great psychoanalyst Sigmund Freud.

Freud used the terms *ego, id,* and *superego* to designate tripartite aspects of the psyche. Over the decades, these terms have given rise to some confusion and numerous interpretations of their meaning. Let's look at these terms and how they relate to your hierarchy of values. You may see why it's wise for you to embrace your true ego, or "I," instead of suppressing or trying to get rid of it.

Many pieces of literature, particularly those influenced by Eastern mysticism, say that having an ego is "bad" and that we need to get rid of it. *Ego* is also often used in a negative way to characterize someone who is arrogant and full of themselves. But originally, Freud used the word *ego* to simply mean a sense of self. Later he revised its meaning to apply to a set of psychic functions including reality testing, governing, planning, information synthesis, intellectual functioning, and knowing. The ego separated out what was real. Freud regarded the ego as the component of the individual that is responsible for dealing reasonably with more objective reality.

Let's look at your value structure or hierarchy of values and how it relates to what Freud called your true ego, superego, and id. We've already seen how your hierarchy of values at any given moment is fingerprint-specific to you. We've already provided you with the tools to determine what this hierarchy means for you.

If you superimpose Freud's language on top of this hierarchy of values, the expression and fulfillment of your highest value is what he would call the true ego—meaning *I, self,* or *true self.*

Some have advised getting rid of your ego in order to be truly spiritual, but I find this advice to be somewhat misleading and confusing. In essence, your true ego is your essential self. It is not your false ego or pride, which is one of the volatile personas and masks that you wear during the day.

When you live in alignment with what you value most; when you are willing to embrace both pain and pleasure; when your highest value is so important to you that it doesn't matter what the obstacles are, because you will turn them into opportunities; when you are able to be more objective and embrace both sides of life—this is the *true ego*.

In my case, I place high value on teaching and learning. As a result, when I'm teaching, researching, and sharing what I discover, I am being true to myself—my true self, my true I, my true ego. I don't think there's anyone who can honestly say they don't want to live that way, even though their lives may be based on completely different values.

When you are living in alignment with your highest values, you are likely to make the biggest difference in the world. You're less likely to be subordinating yourself or conforming to other people; you are being unique to *you* and pursuing what is most meaningful and inspiring to you. As a result, you are likely to be the most disciplined, reliable, and focused in these areas; you will tend to achieve more and emerge as an authentic individual and leader.

This, in my opinion, is the true ego, and there is nothing unwise about living congruently with it. Many people equate the ego with puffing themselves up and pretending they are better or greater than everyone else. However, that is not your true ego. It is your false ego, or pride-filled persona.

If you embrace my definition of the true ego, it stands to reason that if you are trying to get rid of it, you are essentially trying to get rid of your authentic self (or what some theologians called your soul), which is foolish. Even if you meditate and go into a transcendent state that you perceive to be beyond any false ego identification, you will not be able to spend your whole life in that state. Nor will you rid yourself of your true ontological identity. Nor are you likely to make the greatest difference or feel fulfilled: fulfillment also comes through contributing to other people and engaging, interacting, reflecting, and learning.

I'm not in favor of the escapism that is favored by some dissociative spiritual paths. I'm interested in helping you master your life and maximize your full human potential. My primary objective is to give you a strategy to live your life as an authentic self. That's your true ego, and it is not something you need to get rid of. You may want to transcend some of your current false ego-based personas, masks, and facades, but you are not going to get rid of your essential self, and you have no reason to.

The Id

The *id* is what Freud called an individual's impulsive, instinctual, reactive, and animal-like reactions: the hedonic, pursuing, addictive personality, which is in need of immediate gratification.

When you attempt to live in other people's values, often by envying them, putting them on a pedestal, or trying to imitate them, you tend to inject their values into your own life, confused about what is intrinsically highest in priority to you. As a result, you are likely to cloud the clarity of your own mission and purpose, which is your highest value and true identity, and minimize who you are.

When you are not pursuing or not in alignment with your highest values, you are likely to feel unfulfilled and search for immediate gratification in an effort to compensate for that unfulfillment.

This addictive, impulsive, compulsive, immediately gratifying behavior, which often involves fantasy seeking, overeating, purchasing, and consumption, is often an attempt to feel greater about oneself when one is not living according to one's highest values. This reflects a low emotional intelligence.

This immediately gratifying, impulsive, instinctual behavior, which seeks to avoid discomfort and pain and strives to get pleasure quickly, is the *id*.

You activate the id when you transiently attempt to live by your lower values. As a result, you will tend to procrastinate, hesitate, and frustrate. You are likely to doubt yourself and let other people make decisions for you.

You might also find that you are attempting to live according to shoulds, ought to's, and supposed to's, all of which express an imperative language indicating that you are being run externally instead of running yourself. This kind of language is also powerful feedback to let you know that you might have allowed yourself to become disempowered and overpowered by some outer authority that you may be unconsciously envying or admiring.

It is unwise to compare yourself to others. It is wiser instead to compare your own daily actions to your own highest values so you can live authentically by your true essential self, your true ego.

The Superego

Freud described the *superego* as the moralizing force inside of us. By this theory, the superego is a symbolic internalization of parental figures and cultural regulations over the years.

Think of children growing up. In their first year of life, they can do whatever they like and receive unconditional love and support from their caregivers. Once they begin crawling and walking, their parents are likely to say yes and no when they do something that the parent either approves or disapproves of. The parents project these values onto the child, even though they may go against the child's desire-based impulses and instincts (the id), or the child's individual and evolving set of values. As the child grows older, it will often need to make a choice between the true ego (the child's highest values), the id (immediate gratification), and the superego (the externally injected authoritative voice on the inside saying you "should," "must," "ought to," and "have to").

As a result, there is often a three-way dynamic going on: the id wants immediate gratification, the ego wants to achieve what is deeply meaningful to it, and the superego is whispering, "Thou shalt do this" or "Thou shalt not do that."

As the child tries to find its own identity—its true nature amongst its own impulses, inspirations, and its moralizing constructions—it may often experience conflict between what it is "supposed" to do according to the authorities, what it would love to do according to its own true ego, and its id-driven impulses.

The consequence is often frustration and a lack of fulfillment, which lead the child to engage the id. The id, based on a lower value, wants immediate gratification to compensate for the internal conflict and unfulfillment.

Whenever you feel that you are not able to fulfill your highest values, you are more likely to move toward or seek immediate gratification.

The superego is the internalization of the values of outer authorities, which you have injected into your life. This creates internal disorder and conflict between what you truly would love to do, which is your essential self, or your true ego, and this moralizing process or injected superego.

As long as you subordinate yourself to an outer authority, compare yourself to others, put them on a pedestal, minimize yourself, and inject their values, you are likely to have an internal conflict between your true ego and the injected values from outer authorities, and to seek immediate gratification with your lower, value-based id to escape the conflict.

That is partly why very few people become high achievers or great business leaders: they haven't awakened their dormant courage to be themselves; they are worried about fitting in instead of standing out.

How are you going to make a difference by fitting in? You are far more likely to make a difference by standing out.

It is wise not to compare yourself to others, because attempting to live in other people's values will be futile. You will beat yourself up and think you are not disciplined or you don't have what it takes. You will beat yourself up. You are a cat trying to swim like a fish or a fish trying to climb like a cat.

In other words, it is wise to be your true self—the true ego or soul—rather than trying to be someone else.

Your true *you* is yearning to emerge from within; it intuitively wants to express itself and express your genius. It is wise to pay attention to its calling and let it emerge.

Self-Actualization

Let's look at how to live congruently with your true ego.

In 1954, the great psychologist Abraham Maslow published a book called *Personality and Motivation*, in which he described a state he called *self-actualization*.

Maslow said that human beings live according to a hierarchy of needs or values, starting with survival, then moving on to security, socialization, self-esteem, and finally self-actualization.

In short, the individual moves from focusing on the basics, such as food, water, reproduction, clothing, and a secure place to live, to the need for complete fulfillment of their nature as human beings.

Maslow also wrote in great detail about the reality of perceptions versus the objective truth. He believed that self-actualization meant seeing the world as it is and not as you assume it is, and that its magnificence is far greater than the fantasies you impose through your incomplete awareness.

Carl Jung, another great twentieth-century psychologist, spoke of the need for *individuation*, whereby one integrates the pairs of opposites, the unconscious and the conscious. He called this the *conjunction of opposites*.

In the fifth century BC, the Greek philosopher Empedocles said that the universe operates by means of love and strife, that is, attraction, the union of opposite elements, and repulsion, the separation of opposite elements. Empedocles believed that masterful individuals could perceive and act out of love, while less masterful individuals lived in strife because they were polarized in their view. These could be translated into high and low levels of emotional intelligence.

At the level of the true, authentic self, nothing is missing in you. At the level of the soul, the state of unconditional love, the state of authenticity, we have awareness that this is the case. The Gnostics of the second and third centuries AD called it *pleroma*, meaning *fullness*. I was with the Bonpo Lama in Nepal (the Bon is the ancient pre-Buddhist religion of Tibet) when he said, "There's nothing missing; everything is present; it's full."

Yet most individuals feel empty. Here's why.

When you judge another individual and perceive them as beneath you, and you're too proud to admit what you see in them is inside you as well, you have a missing part, or emptiness.

If you put someone above you and you're too humble to admit what you see in them is also inside you, you have a missing part or emptiness as well.

Emptiness is often the result of disowned parts that you haven't yet integrated into your being.

When you put those complementary opposite pairs, or conscious and unconscious parts, together and become aware of both sides synchronously, you're likely to have fullness, pleroma, and a conjunction of opposites. You will be in a self-actualized state, because you're not missing anything. You're full. As stated previously, enlightened love is the synthesis and synchronicity of all complementary opposites.

Equanimity, Transcendence, and "As It Is"

Some refer to this state as *equanimity*. Both philosopher Ralph Waldo Emerson and psychologist Lawrence Kohlberg called it *transcendence*: the highest level of moral reality. They believed that moral actuality is the transcendent state where you transcend the moral hypocrisies of judgments, incomplete awareness, and subjective biases.

The Hindu sacred scripture called the Bhagavad Gita refers to this state as *om tat sat*, or *as it is*.

Mindfulness

The Buddha says the desire for that which is unobtainable and the desire to avoid that which is unavoidable is the source of human suffering; these being the seeking impulses and avoiding instincts of the lower, value-driven id.

Whatever you are infatuated with is unobtainable, because you are no more likely to achieve a one-sided state in life than you are to create a magnet with only one pole.

Nothing is missing. Neuroscience describes this state as integration, synchronization, and simultaneity of the firing of the brain, or gamma synchronicity. I call it self-mastery; others call it a state of synchronicity, transcendence, equanimity, or self-actualization; in Buddhism, it is known as *mindfulness.*

In fact, if you have perfect synchronicity, you experience a eureka moment and have a gamma wave of realization as biophotons are born in the brain. The brain is literally enlightened. In this state of integration and enlightenment, the executive center part of your forebrain governs your behavior with poise.

In other words, when you're self-governed, you are on the path of mastery. You have the pinnacle of emotional intelligence.

Integration and Authenticity

In neuroscience, we know that when you're emotional, lateralization of the cortical brain and autonomic nervous system occurs; that is, they operate in a semidetached way. However, when you're centered, you are likely to have an integration of the brain and the autonomic functions.

The nineteenth-century French scientist Claude Bernard spoke of the *milieu intérieur*, or "internal milieu." In *The Wisdom of the Body*, the American physiologist Walter Cannon wrote about homeostasis. Both concepts point to a stable internal environment within the body. Cannon describes how the body has been created to maintain itself in perfect order, regardless of the ever-changing external environment.

I believe that everything that's going on in your life—physiological, psychological, sociological, or theological—is nothing but a series of feedback mechanisms designed to lead you toward authenticity.

Authenticity is a path of mastery, because the magnificence of who you truly are is far greater than all the fantasies you'll ever impose on yourself.

When you're not living by your highest priority, you are likely to feel unfulfilled. You direct your blood, glucose, and oxygen to your amygdala, the subcortical part of your brain, which avoids predator and seeks prey and avoids pain and seeks pleasure. It looks for immediate gratification, often resulting in compulsive behaviors.

This is not life mastery. This is a sign of lower emotional intelligence.

When you live according to your highest values or top priorities, your blood, glucose, and oxygen go into your forebrain, or prefrontal cortex, your executive center. Whenever you fill your day with the highest-priority actions and do what is most important, meaningful, and inspiring to you, you wake up the part of your brain involved in inspired vision, strategic planning, objectivity, execution of plans, and self-governance. In other words, when you live by your highest priority and feel fulfilled doing what you really love to do, you move along the path of self-actualization. This is a sign of higher emotional intelligence.

Self-Mastery and Values

I speak about values in every presentation I give around the world because if you live congruently with your highest values, you're on the path to mastery.

Whenever you're not on the path of mastery, you tend to polarize yourself instead of synthesizing yourself: you disintegrate instead of integrating.

When you polarize yourself, whatever you are either infatuated with or resent tends to consume your mind. It's often known as *brain noise*.

You may have experienced times when you have not been able to sleep at night because you're preoccupied with what you're infatuated with or resentful of.

Whenever you're emotionally polarized and are consciously experiencing either infatuation or resentment—are impulsively seeking or instinctively avoiding—you're likely to be distracted instead of being fully centered and present.

As I've said earlier, this is when you will tend to activate the subcortical amygdala. Neurology refers to this behavior as Systems 1 thinking. Systems 1 thinking relies on the basic animal part of the brain, whereby you emotionally react before thinking.

Systems 2 thinking is thinking before you are reacting; in other words, where you have governance. Systems 2 thinking is a byproduct of living by priority and synthesizing your conscious and unconscious portions of your mind. It is the key to higher emotional intelligence.

Reason and Presence

Your intuition continually tries to help you become fully conscious. It does this by revealing to your conscious mind what you are unconscious of so that your unconscious becomes equal to your conscious.

When that happens, you have what many philosophers called *reason*, what the ancient Greeks called the *logos*, what the Gnostics called the *pleroma*, what the Buddhists termed *enlightenment*, and what some Eastern mystics called *presence*. All of these paths throughout the ages tend to have a common thread: the brain.

In fact, if you look at the history of this entire journey from the earliest animistic religions, through to the shamans, mystics, and mythologist, then on to religious, metaphysical, and philosophical individuals, and then finally into the scientific age, you can trace the evolution of the human brain.

Your forebrain is doing everything it can to help you have governance, be authentic, and be inspired.

This most authentic state is a transcendental state filled with gratitude, love, inspiration, enthusiasm, certainty, and presence. These are the culmination of an authentic and masterful pathway. It's really a matter of calming down, neutralizing, and reducing any extremes of automatic emotional reactions.

Your Inner Voice

Like many people, you may have wondered if there is any distinction between your neutralizing, intuitive inner voice and your polarizing gut impulse and instinct.

You may have also wondered if it is wiser to listen to one or both of them and even if they are occurring at the same moment. Let's revisit this question in light of our previous discoveries.

There are basic survival reflex responses within you that are similar to those found in animals, which tend to be displayed in certain instances for the purpose of survival.

I'm sure you can remember a moment when you've been infatuated with someone. In that instance, you were likely conscious of their upsides and unconscious of their downsides.

You may not know what happens on a neurophysiological level when you become temporarily infatuated with someone or something. Dopamine, oxytocin, enkephalins, endorphins, and serotonin are elevated in your brain, resulting in a high and a desire to pursue the object of your affection as a predator chases prey. As a result, you will likely associate them with more pleasure than pain and therefore feel an impulse *towards* them.

If you think back to an alternative scenario when you have resented someone or something, you were likely more conscious of the downsides and unconscious of any upsides.

On a physical level, you activated norepinephrine, epinephrine, cortisol, testosterone, osteocalcin, and other transmitters, and initiated an instinct to avoid that individual in the same way that prey avoids predators.

These resulting impulses to seek and instincts to avoid are both registered in your gut or enteric brain in addition to your subcortical amygdala.

Your impulses and instincts are registered in the duodenum, which is a C-shaped section of your small intestine that comes after your stomach. The duodenum has a series of nerve networks, which are sometimes called the *gut brain.*

Your gut brain from your mouth to your duodenum represents your impulse for seeking and consumption. Your gut brain from your duodenum to your anus represents your instinct for elimination or avoidance. In that way, whenever you have an impulse to consume or an instinct to avoid, the gut is activated.

This is most often what people refer to as their "gut impulse" or "gut instinct," which are very different from your intuition. Let me explain further.

Your Intuition

Your intuition is like a homeostat, a negative feedback loop designed to bring the conscious and the unconscious portions of your mind into balance. It helps you become aware of both simultaneously. It helps you integrate and elevate your emotional intelligence.

If you're conscious of the upsides and unconscious of the downsides, your intuition signals potential downsides to bring you back to center—the mean—and extract meaning out of your full existential perception.

This impulse could take the form of a quiet whisper saying, "It's too good to be true," "Watch out for a downside," "Avoid rushing into decisions," or "Keep asking questions before deciding."

That inner voice is your intuition, making you aware of the unconscious downside so you can become fully conscious and aware of both sides synchronously.

In other words, your intuition tries to take the conscious and unconscious splits you create when you judge (which generate survival impulses and instincts), and bring them back into full and integrated consciousness.

To put it slightly differently, your intuition prompts you to see the upsides to what you think are downsides and the downsides to what you think are upsides in order to bring you into homeostasis and balance. In this way, you will be less likely to react. Instead, you will be poised, present, and purposeful, while acting from within on what is most important and meaningful to you.

When you have either an impulse to seek towards or instinct to avoid away, it is due to an activated amygdala, hindbrain, and gut, which sends you into survival mode. By contrast, intuition is a response guided from the prefrontal cortex in your forebrain: the executive center, which leads you back into thrival mode.

The prefrontal cortex, when activated, sends nerve signals down into the amygdala using the neurotransmitter GABA, which is an inhibitory transmitter, and glutamate, which is a stimulatory transmitter, to calm down, govern, or neutralize any impulses and instincts.

This process enables your intuition to whisper to you the upsides of what you see as down and the downsides of what you see as up to bring you back into, homeostasis where you can see the sides you're not seeing otherwise.

Let's recap:

Your intuition is a homeostatic prompting from the advanced part of your brain, the executive center, to bring you back into balance and make you conscious of the unconscious so that you can be balanced and fully conscious, or mindful.

Once you are fully conscious and mindful, you are able to see a situation from a more balanced perspective: not as positive or negative, good or evil, right or wrong, attractive or repulsive, impulse or instinct, but as what it is: neutral.

Being fully conscious and mindful enables you to transcend your animal-like impulses and instincts, which are often emotional distractions, and quieten the noise and chatter in your brain and gut.

As a result, you are far more likely to be poised and see a situation as it actually is instead of being subjectively biased in survival mode, where you will tend to distort your reality, impulsively attracted or addicted or instinctively protecting yourself from a perceived threat.

Your true inner voice acts to guide you to a perfectly balanced state, where you become inspired, grateful, certain of your vision and purpose, vitalized, present, and enthused. It's also where you are likely to feel the most:

- Energized, because in a balanced state, you are most likely to use your energy and resources most effectively and efficiently;
- Authentic, because you are no longer either impulsively looking up to others and minimizing yourself or instinctively looking down on others and exaggerating yourself.

In that way, you can more easily and effectively embrace the magnificence of who you are, which far exceeds any fantasy you may have imposed on yourself.

When the voice and the vision on the inside are greater than all the opinions on the outside, you have begun to master your life.

Your maximum potential emerges when you are being *you*. Whenever you try to be second at being someone else instead of first at being you, you undermine your power.

Your intuition, which is the voice and the vision on the inside, is constantly trying to bring your perceptions back into equilibrium so you can maximize your potential on the planet.

When you tap into the power and wisdom of your voice and vision on the inside (instead of listening to the impulsive and instinctual voices on the outside), you become most present and certain and maximize your emotional intelligence.

If you have to ask whether your inner voice is speaking, it's not, because in that state there's no uncertainty.

Uncertainty emerges when you're exaggerating or minimizing others or yourself: you have unconscious components and therefore have missing information and uncertainty.

The second you listen to your intuition and wake up your inner vision and inner voice, the voice on the inside becomes louder than the ones on the outside. That's your inner voice speaking. It reveals its expression in moments of authenticity.

- That voice will lead you to a state of certainty.
- That voice will lead you to having tears of gratitude.
- That voice will lead you to clarity.
- That voice will lead you to an inspired inner vision.
- That voice will lead you to a state of enthusiasm.
- That voice will lead you to a state of presence and gratitude.

Again, if you have to ask or question whether your inner voice is speaking, your inner voice is *not* speaking.

The secret of tuning in to your inner voice and vision is having a balanced mind and a heart filled with gratitude.

When your heart is metaphorically open wide with gratitude, your inner voice has achieved its aim and has become loud and clear. Your most life-expanding messages can enter into your mind with ease.

In other words, if your heart is filled with gratitude, it is almost impossible to stop your inner voice from speaking clearly and profoundly.

Action Step

Follow the steps below to help you tune into the secret wisdom of your inner voice:

1. Stand relaxed with your hands loosely at your side. Take a few deep breaths. Inhale and exhale slowly through your nose.

2. Tilt your head up 30 degrees.

3. Turn your eyes up another 30 degrees until you are looking forward, inward, and upward.

4. Close your eyelids and let them become relaxed.

5. Think about some event, experience, or individual you are truly and deeply grateful for.

6. Keep reflecting upon what you are truly grateful for until you feel your heart has truly opened up, and you even experience a tear of gratitude or inspiration.

7. Upon attaining a grateful state, now ask your authentic inner voice for any guiding message. Ask: "Inner voice, do you have a message for me at this moment?"

8. When you are grateful enough and you ask for an inner message, a message will clearly come!

9. Write this message down.

10. If your message does not become immediately and clearly revealed, repeat steps 6–10 until it does.

When you are truly grateful, you will receive amazing and inspiring messages from your inner voice. These messages will be more powerful and meaningful than might at first be apparent. When you are grateful, poised, and present, an inner loving wisdom becomes revealed.

If you trust your inner voice and vision and allow this secret intuitive voice to guide your life, you will reduce the imperative language from outer authorities such as "should," "ought to," "must," or "have to." Instead, you will have a voice that says, "This is the path," "Thank you," and "I love you."

When you listen to your inner voice and follow your inner vision, which are congruent with your highest values, when you're unquestioningly certain of your path, and when you have tears of gratitude, it is wise to write any revealed messages and visions down, because it is most likely to be at a moment of authenticity, which is being confirmed by your physiology.

It's letting you know that, in that moment, that one inner voice is the one to wisely follow.

When your true inner voice speaks, you won't have to question it. But when the outer impulsive or instinctive voices speak—the noisy chattering of the brain, and the masks, personas, and facades that you put on in order to deal with your judgments of survival—they cause uncertainty and confusion and can mislead.

As your voice on the inside grows in clarity and strength, so will your inspiration as you listen and follow.

Begin to attune to that inspiring station from within. Listen as it guides you to new levels of creativity and operation. Your true inner voice will put few or no limits on your life. Only the many outer voices of others who allow themselves to live a life of moral hypocrisies and mediocrity will do so.

It is wise to give yourself permission to listen to the secret wisdom and power of your true inner voice instead of your polarized gut impulses and instincts. In doing so, you will be taking a giant step towards strengthening your emotional intelligence, mastering your life and creating an extraordinary future.

When your wise and masterful voice on the inside becomes greater than the many little voices on the outside, a life of great fulfillment, wisdom, and genius can become yours.

8

The Open Heart

'm sure you've often heard the expressions "This opened my heart," or "I have an open heart." It's very common to hear them in personal development programs.

I'd like to particularly focus on my perception of what an open heart is and make a distinction between the true open heart and what others confuse with dopamine and serotonin rushes.

No doubt you have had a moment in life where you have become a bit infatuated after meeting someone. You may have perceived that any resulting relationship would have more advantages than disadvantages, more pleasures than pains, and more positive outcomes than negative outcomes. This perception often stimulates a dopamine rush from your amygdala, the desire center in the subcortical area of your brain, which also elevates the levels of oxytocin, vasopressin, serotonin, endorphins, and sometimes even estrogen.

As a result, your entire body may be flooded with illusive feelings of so-called happiness, safety, attachment, nurturing, and peace, which perpetuate the biased fantasy you create about what could happen in the future, where you are conscious of potential upsides and perceived rewards, and unconscious of potential downsides. It's a kind of irrational exuberance and can make you feel as if you're on a high.

This dopamine and serotonin rush is often confused with an open heart. But actually it is just a transient fantasy.

You may also tend to put that individual up on a pedestal and minimize yourself. You might temporarily set aside what's really important to you—your own highest values—and make sacrifices for the other individual. You may even think you're in love and that you've met your soulmate; you may not want to hear that it's likely to be an infatuation.

A day, a week, a month, or six months later, you may discover that this individual or relationship is not what you thought them to be; you may even feel betrayed by the fantasy that you conjured. What often follows is a time of trying to reclaim higher-priority parts of your life that you have sacrificed or put on hold so you can reestablish equilibrium and take the other individual off the pedestal.

You may go further, moving from infatuation to its opposite, resentment, and begin seeing more negatives than positives, more drawbacks than benefits, more pains than pleasures, and more differences than similarities. You might even resent, despise, or look down on them, perhaps projecting your values onto them and trying to turn them into the individual you think they "should" be. Whereas infatuation often results in a leaning towards, judgment is likely to result in a leaning away from, or avoidance.

Neither of these responses reflects an open heart: they are imbalanced perceptions and a result of a lower and more vulnerable emotional intelligence.

Only when you bring those two extremes into balance—neither looking up at someone nor looking down on them—do you have the opportunity to be grateful, unconditionally loving, and inspired, and feel an open heart. You will then have the capacity to be truly authentic without deflated or inflated facades.

When you minimize yourself and put somebody on a pedestal, and try to get yourself to live in their values, you are not being authentic.

When you exaggerate yourself, look down on somebody and try to get them to live in your values, you are not being authentic.

In other words, whenever you see only the upsides or the downsides, you are imbalanced and become extrinsically run. I'm sure you can remember a time when you were so infatuated with or so resentful toward someone that you couldn't sleep or think clearly because they occupied so much space and time in your mind. Those distracting misperceptions are subjectively biased; they weigh you down, occupy your mind, distract you, and ultimately keep you from having an open heart. They are not an unconditional state, but an infatuation or resentment that is lopsided and conditional.

Your metaphorical heart is able to open only when you have a balanced and unjudging state with pure reflective awareness, where you are not too proud or too humble, when you have no desire to change yourself relative to the other individual and no desire to change them relative to you, and where it's just grace.

If and when you ask the right questions that equilibrate your mind, you can open your heart.

An open heart is an expression of full potential, because you are grateful for life. At the end of your day, if you are not grateful for your day, you are unlikely to have lived by your highest priority. An open heart is the sign of high-priority living and a heightened emotional intelligence.

Give yourself permission to have more moments with an open heart and to be authentic, so you can achieve more, be more, do more, and have more.

Gratitude

You have control of three aspects of your life: your *perceptions*, *decisions*, and *actions*. How do they affect your levels of gratitude?

If you take command of your actions and gear them to your very highest priorities, you'll have the highest probability of having the most gratitude.

When you live according to your highest values or top priorities, your blood, glucose, and oxygen go into the executive center of your brain.

Consequently, whenever you fill your day with your highest-priority actions and do what is most important, meaningful and inspiring to you, you wake up the part of your brain that is involved in inspired vision, strategic planning, objectivity, execution of plans, and self-governance. This is also the part of your brain that maximizes the expression of your enlightened emotional intelligence.

This is also when you tend to feel the most fulfilled, grateful, and able to handle anything resiliently, as opposed to when you're attempting to live by your lower values. In this situation, you are likely to feel that you've been putting out fires all day while ticking almost nothing off your true highest-priority list. When you attempt to live by your lowest values, you'll tend to feel unfulfilled and unappreciative of your day.

So if you're not living by priority, you're likely to be less grateful. However, you can take command of this situation.

You can sit down at any point and decide the quality of day you'd love to have. You can choose to ask yourself equilibrating questions: those that awaken or enlighten your mind to both aspects of your daily events—positive and negative—simultaneously. These questions, when answered, bring your mind into balance. As a result, you can transform your perception of any event into one which centers and empowers you. This is the key to emotional intelligence.

Here are some quality questions you can ask:

- What is the highest-priority action I can do today to help me fulfill my most inspired mission on earth, serve the most people, and fulfill my life?
- No matter what has happened in my life today, how is it helping me achieve what I truly love? How is it helping me fulfill my mission and purpose in life and what I feel is most meaningful?

Asking yourself these questions and linking your perceived current situation with what is most important to you activates the medial prefrontal cortex in the forebrain, which is called not only the executive center but also the *gratitude center.*

As such, you are able to see the hidden order in your perceived chaos; you are more likely to become a master of your destiny instead of a victim of your history.

Taking control of your perceptions and decisions enables you to take control of your actions.

Gratitude enhances all seven areas of your life:

Spiritual. You become more present, caring, and loving when you are grateful.

Mental. You have less brain noise and a clear mind.

Vocational. You become more productive and engaging when you are grateful. You are likely to care about meeting the needs of your customers and employees, with more sustainable fair exchange. You will also tend to have less noise in your brain and live by priority, while also awakening your genius and leadership.

Financial. You become more objective and reasonable. The services that build your financial assets are more likely to appreciate in value than depreciate. If you prioritize your actions and act upon them in accordance with those priorities, it will help you build wealth and serve people in ever greater numbers. You'll grow your wealth potential.

Familial. You are more dialogue-oriented than monologue-projective, as well as patient. Relationships are not meant to be exclusively supportive for you, but instead to help make you authentic, which requires a balance of support and challenge. Ask, how specifically is this other individual—whether supportive or challenging—helping me fulfill my highest values? If you do, you're likely to become more resilient, adaptable, appreciative, and able to say with integrity, "I'm thankful to you. Thank you for what you're doing. I didn't see it initially, but now I do."

Social. You are more caring of others and centered when you are grateful. You tend to display more equity with those you lead or influence, and are more likely to create or lead than follow.

Physical. You are more poised than poisoned when you are grateful, more homeostatic than emotionally erratic. You also tend to be more vitalized, have more energy and physiologically, be more balanced in health. Gratitude and love are still the greatest healers on the planet.

Every situation contains something to be grateful for.
Every situation is neutral until you bias your perceptions and label it otherwise. It inherently has both sides. It is neither positive nor negative until you filter it through your values and narrow it down with your own previously injected moral or ethical label.

Events or actions are neither positive nor negative. There are at least two sides to every event. It is not what happens to you that matters as much as how you perceive it. Daily events can appear to be negative at first glance, and then a day, week, month, year, or decade later, they can reveal their other positive side. The reverse is also true.

The speed at which you perceive both sides is a reflection of your wisdom and the breadth and depth of your awareness. When you perceive both sides simultaneously, you maximize your emotional intelligence and wisdom. As a whole individual, you are neither one label nor another—neither kind nor cruel, neither nice nor mean—but you could be perceived to be one or the other at any one moment. Nothing is missing within you. And you do not need to gain some part or get rid of any part of your self to love and appreciate yourself.

When your highest values in life appear to be supported, you can display one side: "nice." But when your highest values appear to be challenged, you can display the exact opposite side: "mean." But neither side is who you are as a label.

When you see both sides simultaneously, you become grateful for the hidden order within your apparent chaos and express love—the enlightening synthesis and synchronicity of the complementary opposites.

Whatever you label in a one-sided fashion will run your life until you return it to balance and become grateful.

A perfectly balanced mind becomes grateful.

Anything you are ungrateful for becomes baggage, and anything you are grateful for becomes fuel.

Wisdom is the instantaneous recognition that every:

- Crisis is simultaneously accompanied by a blessing;

- Challenge is accompanied by an opportunity;
- Door that is shut is accompanied by an open window.

Wisdom is the synthesis and synchronicity of complementary opposites—which opens your mind.

Love is the synthesis and synchronicity of complementary opposites—which opens your heart.

Philosophy is the love of wisdom and the wisdom of love.

The sooner you see both sides, the wiser and more loving and grateful you become. In addition, when you become fully conscious and grateful, you embrace your conscious and unconscious sides simultaneously.

Your intuition is attempting to awaken you to this wiser state of poise, which is the source of true inspired wisdom, love, and gratitude.

Anything you are not grateful for will run your life.

Anything to which you cannot say thank you will occupy space and time in your mind and run your life until you see both sides equally and become grateful.

In short, gratitude liberates your mind from the emotional baggage generated by unloved judgments.

You can be accountable and diligent on your own and discover the hidden order. And you can generate gratitude through wise and productive self-reflection. Or you can seek assistance from a knowledgeable specialist or Demartini Method facilitator to see the balance and become grateful.

Once you see events as *on the way* instead of as *in the way*, you're set free of the bondage and burden of incomplete and one-sided emotional perspectives.

Operating from a state of appreciation and gratitude is the secret not only of fulfillment, but also of decreasing the frictions and distractions of life. It is an expression of high emotional intelligence.

You have more vitality when you are grateful for all you are, do, and have.

You become less burdened by subconscious emotional baggage when you prioritize your actions and are grateful for events and experiences in your life. You become more uplifted and more enlightened.

True gratitude reflects the state of mental order and poise.

Balanced objectivity is more empowering than subjective, emotionally biased perceptions.

Give yourself permission to see both sides, and liberate your mind and life from unnecessary burdens.

A balanced, grateful mind opens up a loving heart.

Gratitude is the key that opens up the gateway of your heart. This allows the love that resides within to radiate to those you love.

Action Steps for Enhancing Gratitude

Every single day, stop. Reflect. Think about what you could be grateful for. Make it your aim to be appreciative of your life. Acknowledge the magnificent life you experience. It is also wise to prioritize your life and take control of your perceptions, decisions, and actions. In addition, document what you're grateful for on a daily basis.

I am certain that it makes a tangible difference in your life if you take the time to stop and reflect on what you're grateful for and understand how everything is *on* the way and not *in* the way. This daily activity not only reflects a high level of emotional intelligence but further builds it.

Momentum

Another area in which we can apply the insights we've already discussed has to do with momentum. The higher your emotional intelligence, the greater your momentum.

Do you perceive that you are stagnating or not making progress in one or more areas of your life? If so, perhaps you feel that you may be holding yourself back in some way or that you spend a substantial amount of time comparing yourself to what others have or have achieved. You may be wondering why they seem to be building momentum with their achievements while you're treading water.

A feeling of stagnation may not feel comfortable but, like the other emotions I have mentioned, if wisely interpreted, it can provide you incredibly valuable feedback to guide you towards what is truly most important and to a more inspired, fulfilled, and meaningful life. As a result, you build so much momentum that you too become unstoppable.

Here's how.

When talking about momentum, I like to use the analogy of a train. Most people will have seen a train pulling heavy cargo. It starts slowly as it pulls the massive weight behind it before picking up speed or velocity as it goes. You may remember from your school days that momentum = mass x velocity: the mass of the train multiplied by its speed velocity results in its momentum.

It may be helpful to think of that train track as a metaphor for your unique, primary purpose: the objective that's most important in your life or that which fulfills your true highest values.

Again, you can tell your true highest values by finding your most meaningful and inspiring objective. It's an area of work that you love doing that you can't wait to get up in the morning and do. That's your train track path. That's your mission. That's your purpose.

You tend to spontaneously act upon your highest values. But with actions that are low on your list, you tend to procrastinate, hesitate, and become frustrated. You may need someone to extrinsically motivate you to do it or keep doing it.

It may surprise you to know that you tend to be most efficient, effective, and inspired when doing what is highest on your list of values. It's also when you tend to have the least resistance and the most drive, and when your engine becomes unstoppable.

If you live congruently with your highest values, you increase the probability of being clear about your track, your mission, and being spontaneously inspired to act on it without inner resistance. In this arena, you tend to have the fastest speed and accomplish more in less time. In other words, you build momentum.

For example, you may have experienced a time when you set a small goal and achieved it and then immediately set an even greater and more challenging goal. If you achieved that, you may have set a much greater and more unobtainable goal. Your goals keep growing and expanding, and you build momentum to help make you achieve ever more and become unstoppable.

In short, when you pursue something that's deeply inspiring to you, high on your list of values, and achieve it, you tend to want to achieve something greater.

However, when you do something that's low on your list of values, you tend not to want to work so hard. You will probably try to avoid challenges and seek the ease of immediate gratification instead. You're likely to procrastinate, hesitate, and become frustrated with something that takes a lot of effort, because it's low on your value list.

The conclusion is simple: if you'd love to build momentum, it is wise to live congruently with your highest values and keep selectively prioritizing your life accordingly.

Think of a child who spontaneously loves online gaming. He is not likely to need reminders or external motivation to do it; instead, he will jump online and begin gaming every chance he can get. On the other hand, he may not feel inspired to do his homework, read a book, or take part in a sport, so he will tend to find any excuse for avoiding these activities. In other words, his life already demonstrates his higher values or priorities.

The same applies to you: your life *already* demonstrates what is intrinsically important to you, even though you may not think so right now because your perceptions may have become imbalanced and clouded from all of the injected and projected values.

Nevertheless, if you're not consistently moving or building up an accelerated pace towards an aim that's deeply inspiring, you're unlikely to get to a point where your momentum is unstoppable.

Take the boy I mentioned above, who loves online gaming. Many parents know that children who love gaming will play into the early hours of the morning if you let them. As soon as they finish one level, they'll immediately begin the next level, and the next, and the next. They build momentum, they build their skills, they become more confident, and they become unstoppable.

Try to get that child to do homework for a subject he finds uninspiring or unfulfilling, and you will likely have a very different outcome. Why? Because:

He loves doing whatever's highest on his values and becomes unstoppable.

Whereas he tends to stop doing activities that are low on his values and becomes immovable.

I've often spoken about this in relation to students at school. If they can't see how the classes they are taking will help them fulfill what they love most, they're unlikely to become engaged in the content. Getting them to complete the work in these classes is like pushing them up a steep hill, which is the opposite of momentum.

In all likelihood, you know someone who is similarly focused and who will work into the early hours of the morning, not because they have to, but because they're inspired and on a mission.

In truth, nobody goes to work for the sake of a company; they go to work for the sake of fulfilling their highest values. Nobody goes to school for the sake of taking a class;

they go to fulfill their highest values. Nobody gets into a relationship unless it fulfills their highest values.

Every decision you make is based on what you believe will give you the greatest advantage at any moment in fulfilling your highest values.

For this reason, it is wise to prioritize your life by asking yourself: *what is the highest-priority action I can do today that can help me fulfill what's most meaningful to me and serves the greatest number of people?* This is emotionally intelligent.

It is then wise to delegate tasks that are lower on your list of values to those who would love to do and fulfill them.

If you're not delegating lower-priority tasks, you won't be able to spend time on the highest-priority tasks that help you become masterful, build momentum, and be unstoppable.

Give yourself permission to do what's really most important.

You can make a list of every one of your activities in a day, every day, for a week, and look at what you're truly doing. Then you can look at where each one is on the meaning list: How meaningful is it? How productive is it? You may realize that you are majoring in minors and minoring in majors instead of doing what's of highest priority to you. In doing so, you tend to hold back momentum and lower your velocity.

When you do something HIGH on your list of values, your energy goes UP.

When you do something LOW on your list of values, your energy goes DOWN.

Your energy drives your momentum. So if you raise your energy, you're likely to speed up the process, be more effective, efficient, prioritized, and empowered. This fulfills the law of least action and maximum efficiency.

How can do you this? You already know the answer: go through the processes I have outlined in this book, dissolving emotional distractions, phobias, philias, subordinations, and superordinations to other people by asking and answering the questions within the Demartini Method. As we've already found, a feeling of stagnation may not be comfortable, but it can provide valuable feedback to guide you towards a more inspired, fulfilled, and meaningful life, with so much momentum that you become unstoppable.

9

The Hidden Order of the Universe

U p to now, I have discussed the hidden order of the universe in passing, but it's time to go further into this all-important subject.

From the remotest prehistoric times, human beings have been studying the phenomena that surround them and attempting to explain them intelligently.

Primitive mythological explanations were the first signs of the curiosity and anxiety that led human minds to attempt to understand and coordinate the facts that they observed throughout nature. From these initial mythological explanations, religion, philosophy, and, later, scientific methods emerged.

Human beings eventually came to realize that an inherent natural order prevails in every domain.

Only individuals who have devoted their lives to understanding and wisdom can realize what has inspired the great men and women of the past and given them the strength to remain true to their investigations in spite of countless challenges and setbacks. Their genuine cosmic religiosity, with its awe for the hidden, intelligent, and universal order, provided them with the strength and conviction to probe beyond the known into the unknown and make their great new discoveries.

Over time, these inquirers increasingly grasped the number of factors and variables that come into play in the world, to the point where the whole went beyond the reach of exact prediction. In many cases, even the scientific method falls short and breaks down, as when predicting long-range weather patterns or even economic trends. This is due not to any lack of order in nature, but to the enormous number of variables that are operating.

Even so, there is still a hidden, implicate order in the apparent chaos. As soon as inquisitive human beings come to acknowledge the order and regularity of all these factors and variables, they become firmly convinced that there is no room left for causes apart from a divinely organized intelligence.

Divinely Organized Intelligence

Science seeks to reduce the data it analyzes to the smallest possible number of elements so as to rationally unify these diverse phenomena. In this way, it serves to awaken human beings to the hidden, implicate or divine order and the seemingly panpsychic intelligence that underlies the universe.

Anyone who has undergone the experience of making triumphant advances in phenomenology or human behavior is moved by profound reverence for the rationality that is manifest in human existence. Such enhanced understanding can liberate human beings from the shackles of personal fantasies, hopes, and unrealistic desires. It can also enable us to humbly appreciate the grandeur of reason, which is incarnate in intelligently governed existence but in its profoundest depths is inaccessible to ordinary human penetration.

It is enough for me to contemplate the mystery of conscious life perpetuating itself through all eternity, to reflect upon the marvelous structure of the universe which we dimly perceive, and to try humbly to comprehend an infinitesimal part of the intelligence manifested in nature.

Everyone who is seriously involved in the pursuit of science becomes convinced that a spirit is manifest in the laws of the Universe—a spirit vastly superior to that of man, and one in the face of which we with our modest powers must feel humble.
—ALBERT EINSTEIN

True Religiosity

Notice that this great mystery-probing but humble attitude appears to be religious in the highest sense of the word. In essence it constitutes a true religiosity—a deep appreciation for the awe-inspiring intelligence permeating the universe. In this way, true science not only purifies the religious impulse of the dross of its anthropomorphism but contributes to a truly spiritual understanding of the matrix of life. True scientific results are entirely independent of pseudoreligious or moral considerations.

The inspired individuals to whom we owe great scientific achievements were impregnated with the truly religious conviction that this universe is perfect and accessible to a rational striving for knowledge, understanding, and wisdom. If these searchers had not held this conviction strongly, they would hardly have been capable of the untiring devotion that alone enables human beings to attain their greatest achievements.

A Synchronous Universe

Some goals of science are to penetrate further into the mysteries of nature's harmonies; to glimpse the intelligent order which governs this synchronous and elegant universe; to probe deeply into the hidden realities that constitute it; and to apprehend the existence of an ontological order that is beyond mass human awareness. Such discoveries are seldom accomplished immediately: usually they involve long, meticulous, and austere labors.

Inspired individuals untiringly search for this hidden order and these ultimate realities according to their own inclinations or convictions. But they all recognize that the search for truth justifies their patient efforts and constitutes their greatest nobility. This pursuit will eventually awaken the mind to untarnishable wisdom.

If one knew all the factors and variables in this underlying hidden order, one would realize that there is nothing but love.

This recognition constitutes the height of emotional intelligence.

Beyond Happiness and Success

The Declaration of Independence tells us that humans have "unalienable rights" to "life, liberty, and the pursuit of happiness."

This is no doubt the case, but many Americans have taken the pursuit of happiness to the point where it is self-defeating.

Some of the saddest people I know are addicted to the fantasy that it is possible to be hedonistically happy all of the time. They believe it is possible to live a life where there is pleasure without pain, happiness without sadness, and positives without negatives. In other words, a one-sided life.

As previously stated, the Buddha is believed to have said that the desire for that which is unavailable and the desire to avoid that which is unavoidable are the source of human suffering.

As we've already seen, if you're attempting to live a one-sided life where there's just bliss, pleasure, and happiness all the time, without any of the challenges that are inevitable in life, you're likely to become even sadder, because you're in pursuit of the impossible. It is futile to create a one-sided individual, one-sided relationship, or a one-sided life—the illusive philia without its accompanying phobia.

Why, then, do people continue to try to live a one-sided life? Why do they keep trying to pursue the unobtainable and escape the unavoidable?

The answer is quite simple, but it does involve a brief overview of your brain and neurology. As we've already noted, your brain has many levels and layers in it. The two main areas that are relevant here are:

1. The *amygdala* and extended *limbic system* are responsible for most of your emotional responses. The amygdala is also the pleasure center of the brain, which drives you to seek pleasure and avoid pain. It's driven by dopamine rewards. When you're using this part of your brain, you tend to react to the world like an animal—instinctively reacting to avoiding pain and impulsively seeking the next pleasure or dopamine high.

2. The *medial prefrontal cortex* of the forebrain: the *executive center*. This is the most advanced part of the brain, and it distinguishes human beings from other animal species, as it is able to govern and monitor your more primitive impulses and instincts of survival.

For this reason, the forebrain is often referred to as the *thrival* center, *executive* center, or the *evolutionary* center, because this area of the brain is self-governing, is constantly developing and becoming larger and more enhanced in function.

But most people live in a way that develops their amygdala instead of their executive center. This leads to a higher degree of animal survival function and a lower emotional intelligence.

The more primitive part of the brain you are operating from, the more black-and-white and survival-based your thinking, the fewer and less resilient options you have available. You're like an animal that sees prey and runs towards it or sees predators and runs away from them. In other words, you're either in rest and digest or in fight-or-flight survival mode.

In nature, you're consistently likely to have prey and predator. In fact, it's been shown that maximum growth and development occurs at the border of support and challenge, prey and predator, positive and negative. When these pairs of opposites are balanced, you are most likely to maximize your fulfillment.

Think of it this way: if you were to access prey without having to deal with predators, you'd end up being gluttonous and fat instead of fit. If you were exposed to predators without prey, you'd be emaciated and starved instead of fit. But put the two together, and you are likely to have maximum performance and fitness. In other words, you require a balance of opposites to operate at your peak and continue to grow.

Your executive center can override and govern the more hedonistic pursuits, which originate in the amygdala.

The question is, how do you strengthen and develop your executive center so it brings balance and homeostasis and you no longer feel driven towards quick fixes and hedonistic pursuits?

As we've already found, the process begins with your highest values—what's most important to you. When you live congruently with these, you activate your executive center, where you are less likely to be swayed by impulses, instincts, or hedonistic behavior. You are more likely to see both sides of a situation simultaneously and be more objective, balanced, neutral, resilient, and adaptable. You will be able to plan more strategically and execute those plans, thereby empowering yourself. In essence, you will be able to function in a more self-actualized and enlightened manner.

However, if you're doing something that's low on your list of values, you will activate your amygdala. That's when you tend to have a prey and predator mentality, to be more impulsive or instinctual, and to react emotionally before you think. It's also when you tend to be more vulnerable to subjective bias and hedonism. You will function in a more endarkened manner.

When you're living in your executive center, you tend to have long-term vision and you start thinking of your *immortality quotient*. You ask yourself questions like these:

1. What would you love to contribute to the planet?
2. What is the difference you'd love to make?
3. What legacy would you love to leave?
4. What is your unique purpose or inspired mission in life?

When you live by your highest values, you tend to move towards philanthropy. When you live by your lower values, you likely move towards debauchery. Debauchery includes overeating, overdrinking, overpartying, overconsuming, overbuying, overshopping—anything that provides a quick dopamine fix. In doing so, you tend to minimize yourself and have feelings of low self-worth. Overconsuming is a compensation for the state of underfulfillment.

People who buy their first house usually have plenty of storage space. But over the years, they accumulate so many possessions that they can't park their car in the garage because it is full. They watch decluttering programs because their closets are bursting at the seams. These items do not grow in value: they depreciate. Yet these individuals buy even more items they can't afford, living from paycheck to paycheck instead of getting ahead financially.

The lack of a long-term vision and the failure to defer gratification is the cost of hedonism. It's a massive cost in the long-term.

Almost every area of your life is empowered by deferred gratification. While immediate gratification costs, deferred gratification and long-term vision pay.

Financially, if you rely on immediate gratification, keep buying consumables that depreciate, and never make investments that accumulate compound interest, you're likely to be a slave to money all your life. Living paycheck to paycheck is a classic symptom of hedonism.

In relationships, after the initial dopamine fix wears off, you may find yourself looking for that fix outside of your marriage, with a new partner. A few months later, you may be looking for yet another partner to get that quick fix. That's hedonism, and it's highly unlikely to lead to lasting fulfillment.

Your life doesn't have to be an emergency situation where you are constantly in fight-or-flight mode, reacting emotionally to the world on the outside, and looking for the quick fix.

Lasting fulfillment comes from living congruently with your highest values, knowing your highest priorities, and filling your days with them—living a life of design instead of duty.

Lasting fulfillment comes from having a crystal clear vision of your own mission and purpose. In this way, you can live as an angelic human being instead of an animal in the fields, avoiding predators and seeking prey all day long.

The Problem with Success

Donald Keough, the former president of Coca-Cola who led the company through one of its most highly productive and performing eras, once said something that has stayed with me ever since: "I have always been afraid of the word *success*. People, companies, and countries can get into trouble when they start to think they are successful. They get arrogant."

You may have also heard the old saying: pride comes before a fall. You may not know why:

1. *Why* is your perception of success likely to result in your being humbled by others?

2. *Why* does your perception of failure often result in others building you up?

3. *What* you can do to continually center and balance yourself so that you are authentic, purposeful, living by priority, and meaning and mission-focused instead of recognition-dependent and praise-focused?

Whenever you perceive yourself as being successful, you tend to be deflected from your true purpose and allow yourself to perform lower-priority tasks.

When you perceive yourself as successful, you tend to feel a bit elevated with pride. Pride is an exaggeration of self—not your authentic self, whereby you are intrinsically inspired to excel and grow, but an exaggerated self.

As a result, you tend to stop doing the tasks that help you achieve your goals. Instead, you become distracted from your purpose, spending time on lower-priority tasks, splurging and overspending, or taking long vacations. Maybe you have heard the old cliché: "I became so successful I stopped doing what made me so." So-called success can "depurpose" you.

On the other side of the equation, if you think you have failed or are going backwards, it can *repurpose* you. It can inspire you to stop, reestablish your highest priorities, and spending your days living more congruently with them. It can help to repurpose, recenter, and rebalance you.

On certain days around forty years ago, when I was practicing as a chiropractor and had seen lots of patients and earned a lovely income for that day, I would get a little puffed up, perceiving that I was someone special. I then noticed that on those days when I got home, my wife at that time would inevitably humble me!

In my twenties, I was naive about my marriage and began thinking that my wife might be a toxic partner who would criticize me and bring me down. I didn't realize that her criticisms and challenges were not toxicity but instead a caring response to get me back into authenticity and equilibrium. I also began to notice how on other occasions, when I was feeling low and deflated, she would help bring me back into balance by lifting me up and supporting me.

Your physiology, your psychology, your loved ones, friends, colleagues, and society at large are all helping you become the most authentic version of yourself.

- When you inflate yourself and perceive that you're successful, you're not being authentic.
- When you deflate yourself and perceive that you're failing, you're also not being authentic.

However, when instead of chasing success, you're on a mission, neither exaggerating nor minimizing yourself but being appreciative of the opportunity to be of service, you center yourself and are more likely to become truly authentic. This more stable and centered pursuit is the impact of emotional intelligence at its finest.

If you challenge someone's highest values and you're proud and cocky, they're designed to bring you back down into equilibrium, because you're puffed up (above equilibrium).

If you're down and feeling like a failure, they're designed to be supportive and to lift you up, to get you back into equilibrium.

Everything that's going on in your life is trying to get you to be authentic and in equilibrium.

Like the hypothalamic thermostat in your body, which creates sweat when you're warm and shivers when you're cold to keep you at optimal temperature of 98.6 degrees Fahrenheit, your body/mind returns your many daily external perturbations back to homeostasis, as Walter B. Cannon wrote in his 1963 book *The Wisdom of the Body*.

The society around you also acts as a buffer solution to keep you neither exaggerated or minimized, just authentic.

Once I realized this fact, I began looking for ways of self- governing or centering myself instead of relying on the outside world to do so. I was inspired to govern and master my own life so I could be run from within instead of allowing the outside world to run me.

So at the end of each day at work, if I noticed that I was a little puffed up and exaggerating myself, I began asking quality questions to bring balance to my perceptions. Questions such as:

- What did I intend to accomplish but did *not* complete today?
- What members of my team did I *not* thank today?
- What patients did I *not* caringly connect with today?
- What procedure did I overlook today?

The result was that I calmed my pride.

When I completed that little exercise before going home, I noticed that my wife behaved completely differently: she was more stable because I had stabilized myself.

On days where I minimized myself and was down on myself, I began doing the opposite. I would ask myself different questions but with the same aim of bringing balance to my perceptions and authenticity. Questions such as:

- Whom did I serve today?
- Whom did I uplift today?

- What patients' names did I remember today?
- What staff member did I thank today?

Again, I would center myself, and head home to a wife who didn't have to lift me up because I was already in a state of balance.

This was a massive leap forward in my journey to self-mastery. My practice and my relationships became more stable and productive. My emotional intelligence was beginning to grow.

If you don't govern yourself, the world around you will do it for you.

If you don't listen to your internal physiology and psychology and learn self-governance, you're likely to end up being externally governed by your extended family dynamics and sociopolitical or theological rules. If you're cocky, they're likely to bring you down. If you're humble, they're likely to lift you up.

In my case, I realized that if I was initially addicted to praise at work, I'd get slammed at home. However, if I was neutral, didn't puff myself up, and didn't get addicted to praise, I had a more balanced or loving dynamic at home. My wife played out the role of what I was not willing to embrace at work.

The addiction to pride and the aversion to shame are amygdala responses. This is not where maximum performance occurs. In fact, maximum performance and maximum achievement occur at the border of support and challenge, the pride and shame: the authentic self, which sits in the center.

It's why I'd rather call myself a man on a mission than a success or failure. Nor do I label parts of my life as success or failure; instead, I look at them as feedback to bring me back to center—to my authentic self.

I'm not here to promote the idea of success. I'm here to promote the idea of an individual on a mission, living by highest priority, where you're more objective, neutral, resilient, and adaptable—more emotionally intelligent.

If you perceive that you are successful, you can become addicted to success and fear its loss. Many people become depressed when they've been "successful," with the resulting high, but now they can no longer sustain or surpass their previous achievement. They fear its loss and perceive themselves as failures because they're addicted to success.

I'm not interested in promoting a one-sided world. I'm not interested in telling you to *always* be optimistic, positive, peaceful, and one-sided. Frankly, this perspective is not real, and it's not sustainable. It's a fantasy.

The majority of your so-called failure sensations are due to your fantasies of success that did not come true. I've had so many people tell me about their "failed" marriages. To which I reply, "Did you learn something from it? Are you ready to learn from it and take that learning into your next relationship? If so, why do you need to label it as a failure?"

You probably want to be loved for who you are, but you're not who you are when you're proud and cocky or when you're shamed and minimizing yourself.

The ideas of success and failure are labels. They're signs of incomplete awareness about human behavior. They are, when perceived to be extreme, signs of low reflective awareness and low emotional intelligence. When you are fully conscious, you will discover that they are not even two separated poles; they are simultaneously occurring complementary opposites.

Other people's labels mean very little. Other people's opinions of you are not a true measure of your so-called successes or failures. They're simply feedback.

If you're worrying about what other people think about you, you're probably distracted. Instead of comparing yourself to other people, it is wise to compare your actions to what's highest on your values.

I prefer to think of myself as simply a man on a mission. Two people with opposite sets of values will see me simultaneously as a success and failure. But it is wiser to take no credit, or take no blame. Simply focus on your chief aim.

Regrets

Like many people, you may catch yourself thinking, "I wish I had done this," "I shouldn't have done that," or "I really messed up here." You may even believe that you've somehow sabotaged or limited yourself and carry feelings of regret as a result.

Whenever you feel regret, shame, or guilt about something you've done, it likely means that you have expected yourself to do something different from what you did.

You probably also assumed that whatever you did had more drawbacks than benefits, either to yourself or another individual.

Nonetheless, I have yet to see an event or circumstance that has only one side. Every event has two sides.

In fact, everything that's ever happened in your life, to you or from you, has simultaneously both an upside and a downside.

If you focus on the downside without looking for an upside, you'll likely feel regret or resentment.

It is wiser to bring your partly conscious awareness into full awareness where you can simultaneously see both the up and down sides.

Human beings often have a basic assumption that life is one-sided. This results in seeing a negative without a positive or a positive without a negative.

A false positive is seeing something that's *not* there, and a false negative is not seeing something that *is* there.

When you don't live congruently with what you value most, by your highest priority, your blood, glucose, and oxygen flow into the subcortical region of your brain, including your amygdala. Imbalanced perceptions that activate the amygdala give rise to subjective bias and misinterpretation, which are often the source of many of your regrets and resentments.

Once you balance your perceptions, you are able to dissolve the regrets. Note: not "live with" or "come to terms with" your regrets, but *dissolve* your regrets.

Whatever you've done in life is ultimately *on the way* and not *in the way* unless you choose to see it otherwise. That's your own perception.

You have control of your perceptions, decisions, and actions.

If you choose to perceive an event as a nightmare, it can stay a nightmare. But if you find out how whatever you've done or whatever others have done to you has served others or yourself equally, you become liberated.

That's what the Demartini Method is for. It helps you balance your perceptions and dissolve emotions such as rage, guilt, shame, anger, and regret. We've gone through this process in some detail in chapter 3, but as a refresher, we can say that one application of this method involves going to a moment where and when you perceive yourself displaying or demonstrating some specific behavior (trait, action, or inaction) that you dislike in yourself or someone else and that you perceived has caused pain, loss, regret, or resentment.

In other words, you take the time to itemize exactly who you perceive was supposedly affected by it.

The next step involves asking the question: how did it *serve* these other people, or me?

If you choose to never look for the upside, you'll probably live with unnecessary regret or shame.

I often encourage people not to give up too easily when asking themselves this question, because it may seem foreign and challenging if you have become accustomed to playing the victim in your life. I also encourage them not to make any answer up, but look deeply enough to become conscious of the other side of the balanced love equation, thereby bringing their unconscious to full consciousness.

It is wise to hold yourself accountable for balancing out the equation so that you are able to govern and balance your perceptions to become neutral and objective instead of reactive and subjective. The mastery of this balanced accounting helps you govern your emotions and raises your emotional intelligence.

When you're perceiving an event or situation as one-sided, you tend to see more drawbacks than benefits, and you become trapped in a socially imposed moral hypocrisy.

By not seeing the upsides, you unnecessarily trap others or yourself in self-judgment and self-depreciation because they or you never asked, what were the upsides? What were the benefits? How did this event or action serve them or me?

As you become conscious of the benefits, you're going to experience your levels of resentment or regret going down.

I am often asked, what if you perceive that some action of yours has caused someone else more pain than pleasure, more loss than gain, more negatives than positives, and more disadvantages than advantages?

In these instances, my reply is to take the time to stop and look, because there is no event that has one side. There's no event that doesn't have upsides, even though you may currently perceive only the downsides. I do not mean make them up. I mean truly look deeper beyond the initial social assumptions and labels about your action.

The same practice I outlined above can be used in looking for the downsides of what initially appear solely to be upsides.

I have seen hundreds of examples where people have dissolved and balanced their perceptions of apparently unthinkable events.

One that comes to mind is a gentleman who was ransomed for a huge sum of money, which initially appeared to cause a great deal of distress and emotion both for him and his family members. He had been labeled as having posttraumatic stress disorder and found it incredibly challenging to live each day with the high degree of anger, bitterness, and resentment he felt were consuming him.

So I asked him, "What was the benefit to what happened to you?"

He was slightly taken aback and quickly responded that there was absolutely no benefit whatsoever. He asked how I could even think there could be a benefit to what he and his family had been through.

My response, again, appeared to surprise him. I replied that when you have an absolute, moral, hypocritical view about life that's only black-and-white without any gray, you tend to not be adaptable or resilient.

Resilience has a lot to do with the ability to see both sides of a situation.

I asked him to hold himself accountable to looking for the benefits. After a while, he responded that he had been spending far more time with his family since the event.

He carried on thinking for a while before telling me that another benefit was that he had restructured and prioritized his work life so he could delegate more and spend more time doing what he loved before heading home at a more reasonable hour than before.

He then added that his wife had felt inspired to go after what she truly wanted in life because she had realized how quickly life can change and how vulnerable she was having to rely solely on her husband.

After continuing the process and stacking up even more benefits, he realized that the crime, which he had perceived as being so terrible, wasn't so terrible after all.

We were able to dissolve his resentment towards the group of men that kipnapped him, the guilt and shame he carried, and the many emotions that had been weighing him down.

There's no reason to carry unnecessary emotions. Emotions are simply incomplete lopsided awarenesses.

Most people assume that they need to recover from and learn to live with the repercussions of a "traumatic" event. I challenge that model and believe it to be antiquated. I think there's an event that occurred that you have consciously or unconsciously chosen to perceive as being traumatic.

It's not the event; it's your perception of it.

Great philosophers have been saying this for centuries, but many people prefer to run stories about themselves as victims. As a result, they often create a false attribution bias about what other people "did to them" or what they "did to other people." They seem to be more comfortable in a moral, hypocritical world of one-sidedness than in a world where both sides exist.

If you expect yourself to be only nice, never mean; kind, never cruel; generous, never stingy; to only be giving, never taking—in other words, to be only one-sided—you have created a complete moral fantasy and an unrealistic expectation for yourself. Whenever you don't match up to those unrealistic expectations, you're likely to experience regret and shame and feel that you're letting yourself or others down.

Realistic expectations, combined with asking quality questions, can dissolve such unnecessary regret.

I'll probably not ever forget a man coming to my Breakthrough Experience in a catatonic state. I soon learned that he had been named and shamed for a massive explosion at the Phillips 66 refinery in Pasadena, Texas, that had killed over twenty-three people. In brief, he was partly responsible for a part called the valve O-ring. When it leaked, dehydrated, and oxidized, the explosion resulted. At that time, very little could have been done to prevent it, but the company, regulators and media needed a scapegoat, and he was it.

He just couldn't handle the international publicity, together with the fact that he blamed himself. This resulted in his catatonic state, which no psychiatrist or medical professional had been able to break through.

When the time was right and everyone in the seminar was working their way through an individual process, I knelt down in front of him and tried to make eye contact with him. It was as if I weren't even there.

I began listing the benefits and subsequent technological developments that had taken place with the O-ring as a result of the explosion.

Industry's pursuit of safe process design and operation started long before the explosion, which took place on October 23, 1989. Still, at that time, process safety management (PSM) was much different from what it is today. For example, there were no process safety engineers in industrial divisions. Nor were any process safety coordinators directing site compliance activities according to

PSM principles. In fact, the federal Occupational Safety and Health Administration's PSM standard, which revolutionized the uniform application of safe process design and operating practices, was not published until almost three years later. Significant progress from these developments has made industry safer. Through these advancements, countless catastrophic process releases have been prevented, and many lives saved.

I told this man about new systems that had been put into place, enforced periodic replacements of the O-ring to ensure they didn't become oxidized, and the many upgrades to safety protocols and procedures that had been implemented.

I told him how if it weren't for that explosion, further lives would probably have been lost on an even greater scale, and that the overall death rate from injuries and explosions had since dropped. While lives had indeed been lost, lives had also been saved as a result of that explosion.

I continued listing even more benefits until we got to seventy-nine in total, and then I got the whole group involved to stack up as many more as we could come up with. The more we wrote down, the more he began to cry. He finally had some relief from the weight of the shame, self-blame, and regret he had been carrying since the accident. He came out of his catatonic state and returned to function. I later learned that he had returned to work within weeks of his time at the Breakthrough Experience.

Every event is neutral until somebody with a subjective bias labels it as good or bad, terrific or terrible.

As John Milton wrote, "The mind is its own place, and in itself / Can make a heaven of hell, a hell of heaven." It's about perception. I've been teaching people the Demartini Method for nearly four decades, helping them take and cognitively reappraise their perceptions. I have yet to find anything they thought was terrible that we couldn't find the terrific in, or anything they thought was terrific that we couldn't find the terrible in. In fact, each event is neither one nor the other until someone with a narrow view makes it so.

Bronnie Ware, the Australian author of a beautiful book entitled *The Top Five Regrets of Dying*, wrote about the most frequent regrets people mention at the end of their lives. These include having the courage to be more true to themselves, not working so hard, expressing their feelings more, staying in touch with their friends, and giving themselves permission to be fulfilled.

I believe that regrets are unnecessary. If you ask the right questions, become conscious of upsides of which you may have been unconscious, and stack up the benefits, you can dissolve your regret, bring balance to your perceptions, and appreciate your life.

Regrets are simply imbalanced perspectives, and as I mentioned before, you have full control over your perceptions if you ask quality questions to help you balance them.

Retirement

The research around what happens when people retire is fascinating. In many cases, it can accelerate the aging process: a significant number of individuals die as soon as eighteen months after retirement.

By contrast, those who have a clear and defined purpose in life—something that they are intrinsically inspired to do and that keeps their bodies and minds active—tend to live longer, have higher wellness quotients, and experience more fulfilling lives.

I regularly meet business leaders, entrepreneurs, authors, speakers, and performers who are still working and adding value to others into their seventies, eighties, and nineties. Why haven't they retired?

Furthermore, why might you be thinking about retiring at the age of sixty-five (or sooner, if you can afford to)?

For me, a wise place to start is to look at your current job, occupation, or career:

- Are you doing something that inspires you; or
- Is it more accurate to say that you tend to count the days until your next weekend, vacation, or retirement?
- Are you having Monday morning blues, Wednesday hump days, thank God it's Fridays, and week friggin ends?
- Do you work to earn an income so you can pay the bills; or
- Is it more accurate to say that you work because you do what you love and love what you do, regardless of what day of the week it is?

If, like the majority of people, you work mostly to earn a living, is that really how you want to live your life?

When you're doing something that's so meaningful to you that you don't need external motivation to get it done, you're unlikely to think about taking a break. I've been teaching, researching, and writing for fifty years, and I don't have thoughts about wanting to take a vacation from my work. I love teaching and will likely continue to do it seven days a week for the next few decades, because it's what I intrinsically value most and love doing more than anything else in my life.

For you, the tasks will probably be completely different, but the principle and underlying questions remain the same:

- What is it that you spontaneously do on a daily basis?
- Are you doing something you love to do, that inspires you?
- Or are you doing something you perceive that you "have" to do?

There is a scale in life (see accompanying chart). The top of the scale would be something you LOVE to do. This reflects the highest level of emotional intelligence. Underneath that would be what you CHOOSE to do, then what you DESIRE to do, what you WANT to do, then what you perceive you NEED to do, then SHOULD do, OUGHT to do, are SUPPOSED to do, and finally GOT to do, HAVE to do, and MUST do. The last is the lowest level; it is where you are having the most friction, resistance, and feelings of not wanting to go to work or be of service. This reflects a lower level of emotional intelligence. This is in direct contrast to the highest level, when you are inspired and love to work and serve.

Inner Directed (Inspired)

Love to

Choose to

Desire to

Want to

Need to

Should, Ought to, Supposed to

Got to, Have to, Must

Outer Directed ("Despired")

You can often hear this in the workplace when you listen to the words that your colleagues (and maybe even yourself) use throughout the day. At times you will hear, "I should do this," or "I have to do that," and at other times, "I get to do this," or "I can't wait to do that."

The former are employees who likely want to take frequent breaks, while the latter will tend to lose track of time instead of clock-watching until it's time to go home.

It's also interesting to read the research on what happens physically to people who work a sixteen- or eighteen-hour day doing what they love to do. In essence, there tends to be no resulting inflammatory response. The cytokines in their immune system are generally stable, their heart rate doesn't become elevated, and their bodies show few or no signs of distress. Instead, the "healthy" type of stress, known as *eustress*, is invigorating for them.

However, people working the same hours doing work they perceive they *have* to or *must* do often show a resulting increased inflammatory response. In these cases, their pro- or anti-inflammatory cytokines tend to be elevated because they're distressed, which tends to run their immune system down and detrimentally affect their cardiovascular system.

You have two options when it comes to your job: (1) You can do something you really love to do and delegate lower-priority tasks to others, or (2) you can temporarily take the responsibilities of the job you have and link them to what you most value. Do what you love through delegating, or love what you do through linking.

I've helped thousands of people who were uninspired in their jobs identify what they truly value in life and understand how their job description is helping them achieve that through linking. As a result, they become more present, engaged, and inspired by their work.

Once they are clear about their unique hierarchy of values, they can align their work and lives to be congruent with them. They will stop looking for sugar and caffeine highs to keep them awake and no longer need instant gratification and quick fixes to compensate for their unfulfillment.

I cannot emphasize this enough: if you haven't prioritized and organized your life so you can spend the majority of your time doing what you really love to do, now might be a wise time to do that.

If you live your life in such a way that you can't wait to get up every morning and pursue your life's mission and purpose, you may not even consider retiring—not because you lack financial independence, but because you have no desire to retire from the magnificence of your life.

I'm almost seventy years old and I'm still working diligently, not because I need the money, but because I love what I do.

I think that's what real financial independence is: getting to do what you love to do without needing the resulting income. This means keeping your mind and body active, so you don't experience the entropy that tends to follow those who retire without a plan to fill each day with meaning.

As I often say, "If you don't have something to live for, you have something to die for."

I've seen it: I've seen people decay in front of me once they retire and perceive they have nothing meaningful to live for. Pursuing challenges that inspire you reduces the challenges that don't.

One example that comes to mind is a gentleman who ran a major railroad company in America. He sold his company and retired around the age of sixty-nine. In the following months and years, I watched him gain weight, start drinking more, and treat his wife a little more roughly. He became a different human being once he had moved from an inspired life to one with very little meaning, contribution to others, or fulfillment.

So my advice is: if you're going to retire, have a meaningful next step waiting for you.

In other words, don't just retire *from* something, but make sure that you retire *to* something, and something truly meaningful.

Think about the times when you've been the most engaged, inspired, and fulfilled. Those days when you're doing something you love to do and the day zips past because you've lost track of time. Think about the times when you have felt the most fulfilled and grateful because you've made a difference in the lives of others.

That's what I'm interested in helping people do. I love to help them become fulfilled in life.

I want you to be so fulfilled in life that you're not counting down the days to your next weekend, vacation, or retirement.

You really can live an extraordinary life, and you don't need to settle for anything less.

Give yourself permission to take command of your life now so you can live a long, prosperous, meaningful, vital, and fulfilling life in the future. This is the essence of emotional intelligence.

About the Author

D r. John Demartini is a human behavioral specialist and founder of the Demartini Institute, a private research and education institute dedicated to activating leadership and human potential. He's an international best-selling author and business consultant, working with CEOs of Fortune 500 companies, celebrities, and sports personalities. Globally, he's worked with individuals and groups across many markets, including entrepreneurs, financiers, psychologists, teachers, and young adults, assisting and guiding them to greater levels of achievement, fulfillment, and empowerment in many areas of their lives.

For more information about Dr. John Demartini, his live events, and products and services, contact the Demartini Institute on info@drdemartini.com. To view his website, visit www.drdemartini.com.

Printed in the USA
CPSIA information can be obtained
at www.ICGtesting.com
JSHW011018170124
55518JS00002B/8